Centerville Library
Washington **DISCARD** blic Librar
Centerville, Ohio

SENSE & NONSENSE
ABOUT
ANGELS
& DEMONS

D1399559

DISCARD

SENSE & NONSENSE ABOUT ANGELS & DEMONS

KENNETH D. BOA
ROBERT M. BOWMAN JR.

ZONDERVAN®

ZONDERVAN.com/
AUTHORTRACKER
follow your favorite authors

Sense and Nonsense about Angels and Demons
Copyright © 2007 by Kenneth D. Boa and Robert M. Bowman Jr.

Requests for information should be addressed to:

Zondervan, *Grand Rapids, Michigan 49530*

Library of Congress Cataloging-in-Publication Data

Boa, Kenneth D.
    Sense and nonsense about angels and demons / Kenneth D. Boa and Robert
M. Bowman Jr.
       p. cm.
    Includes bibliographical references and index.
    ISBN-13: 978-0-310-25429-4
    ISBN-10: 0-310-25429-9
    1. Angels. 2. Demonology. I. Bowman, Robert M. II. Title.
BT966.3.B63 2007
235'.3—dc22
                                   2007001534

The Scripture quotations contained herein are from the *New Revised Standard Version Bible*, copyrighted 1989, Division of Christian Education of the National Council of Churches of Christ in the United States of America, and are used by permission. All rights reserved. All italics in biblical quotations are added by the authors for emphasis. Biblical quotation from other translations will be noted in the text.

A number of Scripture quotations are also taken from: *New American Standard Bible*, © Copyright 1960, 1962, 1963, 1968, 1971, 1972, 1973, 1975, 1977, 1995 by The Lockman Foundation. Used by permission; and the *Holy Bible, New International Version®*. NIV®. Copyright © 1973, 1978, 1984 by International Bible Society. Used by permission of Zondervan. All rights reserved.

Internet addresses (websites, blogs, etc.) and telephone numbers printed in this book are offered as a resource to you. These are not intended in any way to be or imply an endorsement on the part of Zondervan, nor do we vouch for the content of these sites and numbers for the life of this book.

All rights reserved. No part of this publication may be reproduced, stored in a retrieval system, or transmitted in any form or by any means—electronic, mechanical, photocopy, recording, or any other—except for brief quotations in printed reviews, without the prior permission of the publisher.

Published in association with the literary agency of Wolgemuth & Associates, Inc.

Interior design by Mark Sheeres

Printed in the United States of America

07 08 09 10 11 12 • 15 14 13 12 11 10 9 8 7 6 5 4 3 2 1

CONTENTS

Part 4 ▪ THE DEVIL AND HIS ANGELS

ABBREVIATIONS

AGJU   Arbeiten zur Geschichte des Spätjudentums und Urchristentums
HCSB   Holman Christian Standard Bible
KJV   King James Version
LCC   Library of Christian Classics
NASB   New American Standard Bible
NET   New English Translation
NIV   New International Version
NKJV   New King James Version
NRSV   New Revised Standard Version
NWT   New World Translation

PREFACE

A good case can be made for thinking that there have been enough books written already about angels and demons. We would refuse to add to the pile except for one thing: so much of what has been written is nonsense.

That may sound intolerant or ungracious, but putting it any milder would obscure the point. There are people who report talking to angels for hours on end, yet the "message" these angels bring sounds suspiciously similar to the pop psychology of the day. Books promise their readers contact with angels on a regular basis, bringing power, healing, prosperity, forgiveness, comfort, revelations, spiritual transformation, and daily guidance of the sort usually associated with horoscopes. Even books that don't make such hyped promises often regale us with one anecdote after another about angelic visitations, leaving all sorts of false impressions about what people can expect from angels. Books about demons likewise often contain generous amounts of drivel, if not dangerous notions. Demons get blamed for everything bad, and even some things that are not bad at all. At the other end of the spectrum, some people are skeptical about the existence of angels or demons.

Our goal in this book is a modest one: to help you think clearly and critically about the subject of angels and demons. To that end, we look at a variety of beliefs about these invisible creatures. Although we are Christians, we identify some nonsense coming from Christian as well as non-Christian sources. In that respect, we are "equal-opportunity offenders": we think nonsense should be exposed wherever it may be found, even in our own religious backyard.

Much of this book will focus on getting a clearheaded understanding about just what angels are. Before we begin, though, we should point out that the word *angels* has at least three meanings.

(1) Sometimes by "angels" people mean any sort of created spiritual being, including angels in heaven with God and the "fallen" or wicked angels, also called demons. (2) Sometimes the word "angels" refers only to the good, heavenly angels, in contrast to the demons (as in our title's reference to "*angels* and demons"). (3) Less common today, but still seen occasionally, is the use of the word "angels" to refer to a specific rank of heavenly beings whose main task is the communication of messages (because the Greek word *angelos* meant "messenger"). It will usually be obvious from the context which meaning applies.

Without further ado, then, let's start sorting out sense and nonsense about angels and demons.

PART 1

HOW TO THINK ABOUT ANGELS

Chapter 1

ANGELMANIA!

A lot of people get carried away with angels, but we still
need to think about them.

An awful lot of what people say about angels is nonsense.
For centuries people have entertained the wildest speculations about both angels and demons. We've all heard the question
about how many angels can dance on the head of a pin, a question
that for many of us epitomizes the fanciful, irrelevant nature of
doctrine. "Who knows and who cares?" we think when we hear a
question like that.

A Brief History of Angelology

The study of *angelology* (the doctrine of angels) played a surprisingly big role in medieval thought. The basic textbook on the subject was a book called *Celestial Hierarchy*, purported to be authored
by Dionysius, an Athenian converted to faith in Christ through the
preaching of the apostle Paul (Acts 17:34). Medieval theologians
generally accepted the book's claim at face value and consequently
treated it as an authoritative guide to what the apostles believed
about angels. Modern scholars, though, uniformly agree that the
book was written centuries later, and so they refer to its author
as "Pseudo-Dionysius." We'll talk more about this angel book in
chapter 12.

Angelology reached its heyday in the thirteenth century, when
Europe's most brilliant minds wrote extensively on the subject and

university students (e.g., at Paris) were required to take courses in it. Two thirteenth-century theologians epitomized that era's interest in angels and developed the most thorough, sophisticated systems of angelology the world has ever seen. Thomas Aquinas (1225–74), widely regarded as the most brilliant Christian theologian and philosopher during the long stretch of centuries from the fall of the Roman empire to the Renaissance, was known as the Angelic Doctor. A member of the Benedictine Order, Aquinas devoted a good bit of his classic, multivolume work *Summa Theologiae* to angels.

Aquinas's older contemporary Bonaventure (1217–74) was called the Seraphic Doctor because he was a member of the Franciscans. They were known as the Seraphic Order because Christ was reported to have appeared to Saint Francis in the form of a seraph. Bonaventure himself was said to have been visited by an angel, and he interpreted the sixth angel of the book of Revelation as a reference to Francis.[1]

Aquinas, Bonaventure, and other theologians of the time sought to answer a number of perplexing questions about angels. They tried to explain when and where the angels were created, to what rank of angels the Devil had belonged and why he fell, what each of the different kinds of angels does, and similar minutiae. Some of the lesser lights of the period got especially carried away with speculations on such matters. One thirteenth-century cleric, Albert the Great, opined that there were 266,613,336 good angels and exactly half as many fallen angels — 133,306,668 in number — making the total number of angelic beings 399,920,004.[2] Most medieval theologians, however, including Aquinas and Bonaventure, argued that the number of angels is incalculable and admitted that some things about angels were beyond our ability to attain certain knowledge.[3]

MORTIMER J. ADLER

The myth that intense discussion focused on the number of angels that might dance on a pinhead is simply one of the many modern inventions contrived to make a mockery of mediaeval thought.[4]

In fairness, we should acknowledge that medieval theologians did some good thinking about angels and demons—and contrary to popular myth, they did *not* debate the angels-dancing-on-a-pin question.[5] They did debate whether angels occupy space at all and whether angels move in or through space. These questions may also seem arcane, and they probably go beyond what we can know with any certainty, but they were serious questions that had some bearing on the larger question of just what kind of beings the angels are.

In reaction to the excesses of late medieval theology, John Calvin, one of the leading Protestant Reformers of the sixteenth century, threw buckets of cold water on angelology. Calvin urged Christians to be wise and "leave those empty speculations which idle men have taught concerning the nature, orders, and numbers of angels."[6] To this day angels are given much more "press time" in Catholic theology than in most Protestant theological traditions. That hasn't stopped some Protestants, however, from exercising their own imaginations on the subject of angels.

The scientific revolutions of the past four centuries actually began to erode belief in spiritual beings among educated people, especially in the nineteenth and much of the twentieth centuries. Belief in angels—let alone adherence to extravagant views about them—came to be regarded in many circles as superstitious nonsense. As late as 1982 Mortimer J. Adler, a prominent American philosopher who actually believed in angels, commented, "It would appear to be a dead subject, of interest only to historians, and of limited interest even to them."[7] Even in 1990 Malcolm Godwin could write a book declaring angels to be "an endangered species."[8]

How quickly things change. The year that Godwin's book was published, interest in angels, which was already building, exploded in America. On the leading edge of the angel craze was Sophy Burnham's *A Book about Angels*,[9] one of the bestselling books of 1990. A

STEPHEN F. NOLL

People are now talking about angels. But does anyone *think* about them seriously?[10]

Gallup study reported that belief in angels among US teenagers rose from 64 percent in 1978 to 76 percent in 1992.[11] In 1993 *Touched by an Angel* (remarkable, it should be noted, for its restraint in its portrayal of angels) began its ten-year run on prime-time network television. Angelmania was upon us.

The media seemed to reach its angel saturation point toward the end of the 1990s, but popular interest in angels remains high. According to Barna Research, by the year 2000 over four-fifths of Americans believed that angels exist and that they influence people's lives.[12] Belief in angelic influence, of course, is what makes this subject important. If angels do exist and influence human lives today, what can we know about them?

The Roads Not to Be Taken

Two all-too-easy approaches to this subject seem to grab many if not most people. The first easy way is to take an attitude of uncritical acceptance toward any information about angels that comes our way, or at least any that appeals to us. Angels are fascinating and mysterious creatures, and any insight we can gain about them can be exciting. Unfortunately, it is impossible for everything people say about angels to be true. Angels are reported to have communicated revelations from God that started religions as diverse as Islam and Mormonism. Some angels are said to have announced that only one religion is true, while other angels are said to have informed the world that all religions are valid. Some people believe angels protect everybody; others believe angels only protect people who have the right kind of faith.

Not everyone sees it this way. Many of the most popular writers on angels take the view that anything goes. Terry Lynn Taylor tells her readers, "Get used to the idea that there are no 'right' or 'wrong' opinions — only opinions that are different or similar. There are no right or wrong religions, no right or wrong ways to God."[13] Frankly, this is nonsense — and we mean that quite literally. Taylor's claim that there are no right or wrong opinions or religions is itself an opinion; and it is either right (something we should accept) or wrong (something we should not accept). More precisely, it is either true or false. The opinion that no opinion is right or wrong is nonsense because, if it's right, it's neither right nor wrong![14]

Later in the same book, Taylor asserts, "The best measure of truth is what you feel in your heart is true."[15] On a surface level, it is contradictory to claim that there are no right or wrong opinions *and* that there is something called truth. However, both claims amount to the same thing: you should accept whatever you feel in your heart and not concern yourself with whether it matches with someone else's "opinion" of what is right or wrong. This is a prescription for self-delusion. We are, of course, under no obligation to accept the opinions of others. However, if we want to know the truth, we will listen to others and put our *own* opinions to the test. What we "feel in our hearts" might, after all, turn out to be false.

Similarly bad advice is Karen Goldman's suggested approach to reading her own book on angels: "Eat it all up, and spit out whatever you don't want."[16] We need to be more discriminating in the restaurant of ideas than to swallow whatever tastes good.

We also need to avoid uncritical, gullible thinking about the Devil. Belief in the existence of the Devil and his helpers, the demons, is also widespread, though not as prevalent as belief in angels. But some people give the Devil entirely too much credit. They blame almost everything bad that happens—including anything bad that *they* do—on him. Rather than viewing the Devil as a simple explanation for everything that goes wrong, we need to find a way of recognizing what is truly demonic and what is the result of other factors.

> It is impossible for everything people say about angels to be true.

The other oversimplistic attitude that some of us are inclined to take toward angels and demons is an unmeasured skepticism. It is understandable for thinking persons, disturbed by the excesses of popular teaching and lore about angels, to view the whole idea with what the mid-twentieth century Swiss theologian Karl Barth called a "weary shrug of the shoulders."[17] It is easier to deny the existence of angels altogether, or at least to deny that we can know anything about them, than to sort through all of the conflicting and hyped claims.

The easiest path, though, is often not the right one. If angels are poised to help us, we may be missing out if we don't pay attention to them. And if demons pose a threat to us, we ignore them at our peril. The smart thing to do is to find out what we can about both angels and demons and determine what, if any, change in our lives we ought to make in the light of that knowledge.

In this book we will be taking a hard look at many popular notions about spiritual beings. We will not try to address every controversial question about angels and demons; instead, we will be glad if we succeed in setting forth a good, helpful way of thinking about the subject. Our goal is to discern the truth about angels and demons and to dispel much of the nonsense about them that is so prevalent in our society. Our method is to *think critically*—neither gullibly accepting nor casually ignoring what others say, but giving careful, reflective consideration to the subject. Some of the things that we have learned about angels and demons, frankly, surprised us. They may surprise you as well.

SENSE
You can't believe everything you hear about angels.

NONSENSE
You can just ignore the whole subject of angels.

Chapter 2

THE SKEPTIC'S GUIDE TO SPIRITS

You can believe in angels and other spirits — and keep your brains, too!

In this chapter we are going to answer the two most common objections to belief in angels, demons, or other spirits. Our goal here is straightforward: to show that belief in spiritual beings is not unreasonable.

Angels: Products of Uncritical Minds?

Skeptics generally dismiss all accounts about angels as superstitious nonsense, to be classified along with alleged sightings of Bigfoot, the Loch Ness Monster, alien spacecraft, and Elvis. And they have a point. There are so many stories about people claiming to see so many things, and, as we have already admitted, they can't all be true. It isn't hard to see why tough-minded thinkers fold their arms and insist that they won't believe such things unless they see them with their own eyes.

Let's go a little deeper. Suppose you're flipping through the channels on your TV and stumble across a televangelist who claims that he had a visitation from an angel. If you're anything like us, you're going to question his story. You're going to doubt. In the face of such a claim, it will seem more reasonable to conclude that the televangelist was (1) *deluded* by some hallucination, (2) *duped* by someone playing a trick on him, or (3) *deceiving* the public, rather than to conclude that he really saw an angel.

But is it reasonable to think that *all* accounts of angelic encounters can be explained in these ways? We don't think so. It simply isn't accurate to treat belief in angels as necessarily associated with gullibility, superstition, or religious hucksterism. Some of the finest minds in the history of the world—including some great thinkers of our own time—have accepted the existence of angels. The enormous success of the natural sciences during the past couple of centuries managed only to erode belief in the supernatural to some extent, not to eliminate it. The reality of angels continues to be affirmed by well-educated men and women who have no vested interest in the idea and who do not exhibit signs of superstition in their general thinking and behavior.

Consider, for example, Mortimer J. Adler, whom we quoted in the first chapter. He served for decades as the Chairman of the Board of Editors of the *Encyclopaedia Britannica* and was the driving force behind the publication of the Great Books of the Western World. He was one of America's premier philosophers and educators from the 1940s until his death in 2001. Adler had no stake in promoting belief in angels; he didn't even profess to be a Christian when he wrote his book *The Angels and Us*. (He was baptized a couple of years after the book was published.) We offer the late Professor Adler as "Exhibit A" that belief in angels is not incompatible with being a highly educated, disciplined thinker.

Angels: Persons of Bodiless Minds?

The second objection to believing in angels is that angels by definition are minds without bodies. (We agree with this definition, by

MORTIMER J. ADLER

The incorporeal and the invisible may be unimaginable by us, but they are not unthinkable or unintelligible. Angels are no more incomprehensible than minds or intellects are, whether embodied or not.[1]

the way; see chapter 6 for the details.) But the concept of a mind without a body, skeptics complain, is incoherent or unfounded or both. By *incoherent* skeptics mean that they don't get it; they find the concept unintelligible. By *unfounded* they mean that they don't see any good reason for holding to the concept.

The cogency of the claim that the concept of a bodiless mind is incoherent depends on what one means by incoherent. If one means that the concept makes no sense, we disagree. Most people, in fact, seem to have little or no trouble grasping the concept of a mind that is not dependent on a body. In most cases what skeptics mean is that they have difficulty understanding how a mind can function without a body. This we freely admit. Our experience as minds is limited to the bodily world, making it difficult if not impossible to understand how a mind can function apart from that world. But that doesn't make the concept of a bodiless mind irrational. It is not irrational to admit the existence of things we can't fully understand.

Whether or not there are good reasons to believe in the existence of bodiless minds will depend on one's total worldview. As we have explained in another book, we find many compelling evidences for the existence of God, who is the ultimate bodiless Mind.[2] There's a reason why most people who believe in an all-powerful, personal God who created everything don't have a problem believing in the existence of angels. If God exists and can make the universe out of nothing, creating angels should be a snap.

> It is not irrational to admit the existence of things we can't fully understand.

Another example of bodiless entities or minds without bodies is the souls of human beings after death. If some immaterial part or aspect of a human being exists after death—call it the mind, the soul, the spirit, or whatever—that would be another example of a bodiless mind. Again, there are good reasons to believe that such postmortem existence is a reality,[3] just as there are good reasons to believe that we have souls in the first place.[4]

The bottom line is this: if you don't believe in God, may we respectfully suggest that you slip a bookmark in this book right now and go do some serious wrestling with that question? Frankly, it's a much, much more important question than whether angels exist. (You can always come back and finish this book later!) If, however, you're satisfied that God exists, then you really should not have any trouble with the idea that angels might exist.

SENSE

If you can believe in God, you can believe in angels.

NONSENSE

Belief in angels is superstitious and irrational.

Chapter 3

NEVER ASK AN ANGEL FOR HIS RÉSUMÉ

Angels are not the best source of information
about angels.

The conventional wisdom is that if you want to know something about someone, you should always get it straight from
the horse's mouth. So it would seem obvious that "the best teachers
about the nature and work of angels" would be angels themselves.[1]

Not so. There are at least four reasons to be cautious about basing
one's views regarding angels on information supposedly originating
from the angels themselves.

Not All "Angels" Are Alike

Perhaps the first and most obvious reason for not looking to angels
for our angelology is that the "angels" don't all agree. Not only are
angelic visitations reported in many different and conflicting religions, but the religions and cultures of the world tell stories about
all sorts of spiritual, supernatural, and otherworldly kinds of entities. These alleged entities include devas (demigods of Hindu lore),
elemental spirits, fairies of all kinds (such as elves or pixies), jinn
(or genies), and many others.[2]

Angel enthusiasts have at times acknowledged this point, though
without recognizing its cautionary side. The authors of the popular book *Ask Your Angels* (the title of which is itself telling) urge

their readers to learn to "tune into another channel on a higher frequency, the voice of your angel" — and they admit you might have
other kinds of encounters as well. "Once you tune into the angels,
you may find yourselves receiving other stations as well — voices of
guides, extraterrestrials, and nature spirits."[3]

Before we take any or all such stories at face value (and one can
find people who do take each of these categories of beings with
great seriousness), we might want to look for a more reliable source
of information about the supernatural.

Some Reports about Angels May Be Wrong

We must also consider the possibility that some of the stories being
told about angels or other spiritual beings are simply false. Human
beings who report seeing an angel or a fairy or some other kind
of otherworldly creature might be delusional, lying, or simply mis-
interpreting their experience. By no means are we saying that *all*
such stories are false. But even if only some of them are erroneous,
we have to find a standard for sorting out which stories are true and
accurate and which ones are not.

The "Angels" Could Be Lying

Moreover, even if a story of such an encounter is reported accu-
rately, it may be that the "angel" lied. Good angels, of course, can
be counted on not to lie. But we have no reason to assume that all
angels are good — and if some angels are bad, it is reasonable to
suppose that such evil beings would lie about themselves.

Again, most if not all cultures and religions acknowledge the
existence of evil spirits of one kind or another. If demons exist, we
need to make sure that we know which spiritual beings are angels
and which ones are demons — and it is unlikely in the extreme that
they wear color-coded uniforms or carry ID cards. The prudent

JAY STEVENSON

In the real world of angel watching, however, there are no rules. Angels
are in the eye of the beholder.[4]

thing to do, then, is to find some reliable way of testing an angel's claim before accepting anything he says.

Angels Don't Write Autobiographies

Finally, at least some venerable traditions about spiritual beings indicate that we should not expect angels to provide much information about themselves. Billy Graham has called angels "God's secret agents."[5] The metaphor is helpful in many ways, not the least of which is to suggest that their job description precludes angels from saying much about themselves.

According to the traditional beliefs of Jews, Muslims, and Christians, when angels speak to humans they communicate messages from God. The very word *angel*, in fact, derives from the Greek word *angelos*, which means "messenger." Just as we expect human messengers to give their boss's message and leave, so we should not

> We have no reason to assume that all angels are good.

be surprised to learn that God's angels give human beings the message God sent them to deliver and do not say much at all about themselves.

For all these reasons, then, we should not expect to gain a clear, reliable understanding of angels and demons from the angels themselves.

SENSE

Some of what angels are reported to say may be true.

NONSENSE

Angels can be trusted as reliable sources of information about angels.

Chapter 4

ALL YOU NEED TO KNOW ABOUT ANGELS

The Bible tells us everything we need to know about
angels and demons.

If anyone might have been expected to appeal to personal experience about matters of religion or spirituality, it was Jesus. Even radical and skeptical scholars agree that Jesus was a man marked by his own deeply profound experience of God. Yet when Jesus engaged others in conversation about controversial questions of faith, he routinely appealed not to his own experience but to the Scriptures.

A particularly telling example comes from Jesus' discussion with some Sadducees. The Sadducees were the priestly "party" in first-century Judaism that controlled the temple. They were also the theological liberals of their day, questioning a number of doctrines taught in the later parts of the Old Testament as well as by the Pharisees (the rabbinical wing of Judaism). For example, the Sadducees didn't believe in angels, and they didn't believe in a future resurrection from the dead (see Acts 23:6–9). Regarding such matters, Jesus told the Sadducees, "You are wrong, because you know neither the scriptures nor the power of God" (Matt. 22:29).

Why Believe the Bible?

Unfortunately, many people today have serious reservations about basing their beliefs about any subject—whether angels or anything else—on the Bible. We have discussed this question in a more general way elsewhere.[1] Here we will restrict ourselves to making some observations about the credibility of the Bible in what it says about angels and demons.

(1) *The Bible lacks speculative and frivolous details about angels.* It offers no exact count of the number of spiritual beings. Descriptions of angels when they visit humans are short (the descriptions, not the angels!) and contain almost no details about their physical appearance. In marked contrast to angel literature of almost every age and culture, the Bible exhibits considerable restraint in its statements about angels. Scripture is similarly reserved in its comments about the Devil and his demons; in fact, absolutely no description of the Devil's appearance is ever given in the Bible.

(2) *Angels are of subordinate interest to the Bible's most important and dramatic accounts.* Scripture never presents angels as of any interest or significance in and of themselves; they are mere messengers or servants of God carrying out his orders while the real action centers on other things. Daniel saw angels, but the message of his book was not that angels came to him but that God is sovereign over the kingdoms of this world and that he would eventually bring the kingdom of God to earth.

The Bible names only two angels — Michael and Gabriel — and tells us little about either of them.[2] The women who visited Jesus' tomb early Easter morning saw angels there, but the good news that the women passed on to Jesus' male disciples was not that angels were about but that Jesus was alive. The incidental as well as reserved nature of the biblical angel reports gives them a credibility often missing in extrabiblical angel stories.

(3) *The most important angel reports in the Bible are part of historically supportable events and claims of the Bible.* A number of angelic visits are closely linked to God's promises to Abraham and Jacob that they would become the fathers of a multitude (especially

KARL BARTH

Holy Scripture gives us quite enough to think of regarding angels.[3]

in Gen. 18 and 32). We cannot verify historically that the angels appeared to Abraham and Jacob, but we can verify without even trying that God's promises to them have been stupendously fulfilled.[4] The Gospel reports of the angels at Jesus' empty tomb are credible once one recognizes that the empty tomb is a fact and that the more stupendous miracle of the moment, the resurrection of Jesus, is well supported historically.[5]

To a thoroughgoing, committed skeptic, no amount of evidence could ever make any reported supernatural occurrence credible. But for those who are open to the possibility of the supernatural, the Bible is by far the most credible source of information about angels of all time.

Thinking Biblically about Angels

To say that the Bible is the best, most reliable source of information about angels — and, for the Christian, the final authority on the subject — does not mean that we are simply supposed to repeat biblical accounts about angels. Nor are we suggesting that we should never listen to reports about angels from outside the Bible. Rather, what we are urging is that we ought to think *biblically* about angels and demons. Let's quickly unpack what that means.

(1) *Any story or teaching about angels or demons that contradicts the Bible should be rejected.* Remember Jesus' message to the Sadducees: If you don't know what Scripture says, you are liable to fall into error. The Bible is our first line of defense against nonsense about angels and demons.

(2) *We should seek to know and understand whatever the Bible teaches about angels.* According to the apostle Paul, "All Scripture

MARTIN LUTHER

From the beginning of my Reformation I have asked God to send me neither dreams, nor visions, nor angels, but to give me the right understanding of His Word, the Holy Scriptures; for as long as I have God's Word, I know that I am walking in His way and that I shall not fall into any error or delusion.[6]

is inspired by God and is useful for teaching" (2 Tim. 3:16). In other words, whatever we can learn from the Bible about angels and demons will be helpful to us in some way.

(3) *We should not expect people to believe any claims about angels or demons that are not solidly based on the Bible.* Another way to make the same point is that, as Barth put it, Scripture tells us everything we really need to know about angels. Any speculations about angels that cannot be substantiated from the Bible may be ignored. Of

> The Bible is our first line of defense against nonsense about angels and demons.

course, as we have already pointed out, if those speculations contradict the Bible they should actually be rejected.

The "flip side" of this last point is that beliefs about angels or demons that can't be proved or disproved from the Bible may be viewed as acceptable but not important. Such ideas may be entertained and discussed, but it would be wise not to build anything critical on them.

(4) *We should use all our knowledge and reason to understand more fully what the Bible says about angels and demons.* Using science or philosophy to try to debunk the Bible is not a good idea; using these or other disciplines to gain clearer insight into the Bible is perfectly appropriate. As we explained in chapter 2, you don't have to suspend critical thought to believe in angels.

SENSE
The Bible is the one truly reliable source about angels and demons.

NONSENSE
Basing one's beliefs about angels on the Bible means not thinking critically about them.

PART 2

WHAT ANGELS ARE AND ARE NOT

Chapter 5

LUCY IN THE SKY WITH DEMONS: ARE ANGELS ETS?

Angels are not extraterrestrial beings far advanced beyond us in evolution.

What are angels? Many different theories have been advanced as to the real nature of angels, but one is peculiarly *modern*. It is the notion that angels are beings from another planet (or other planets) that are simply further along in their evolution than we are.

The idea that angels are really advanced extraterrestrials takes different forms, but the usual version is that people in biblical times were visited by such interplanetary travelers and interpreted those visits according to their prescientific, supernatural worldview. Such visitations, which were apparently rare for many centuries, suddenly became numerous beginning in the late 1940s. Many people believe that at least some UFOs (Unidentified Flying Objects) are spacecrafts piloted by beings from other planetary civilizations that are highly advanced technologically and in other ways in comparison to our own human race. On the supposition that such visits also occurred in the ancient past, some UFO enthusiasts have concluded that these ancient visitors to Earth (whose abilities obviously were incomprehensible to such "simple folk") were interpreted as supernatural beings.

If it sounds like we're talking science fiction here, we are! The general story line we have sketched above functions as the premise of science fiction films and television programs. Sometimes the story is about aliens who came to Earth posing as gods (as in the film *Stargate* and the TV series *Stargate SG–1*). In some stories human beings in the future visit more backward planets and are inadvertently mistaken for gods or angels (a premise used repeatedly in *Star Trek*).

Angels: The UFO Connection

If the idea of angels as space travelers were merely a premise of entertaining science fiction, it would be harmless enough. When it becomes the premise of a religion, though, something has gone seriously wrong. In many of these UFO cults the leaders claim to convey messages received (e.g., telepathically) from these "angels" (often called "space brothers" or some other exotic designation).

One of the more influential UFO cults is the Unarius Academy of Science, founded by husband and wife Ernest and Ruth Norman. According to the group's website, Mrs. Norman had a psychic revelation in 1975 that she and her late husband were reincarnations of ancient contactees Isis and Osiris, "overshadowed by the Archangels Raphiel and Uriel."[1] Earth is being prepared spiritually to be inducted into an "Interplanetary Confederation" consisting at present of thirty-two other planets. Help comes not only from psychic contact with beings from these other planets, but also from psychic communications from departed earthlings, such as 1950s actor James Dean and *Tarzan* author Edgar Rice Burroughs.

Another important UFO cult is Urantia, which has as its centerpiece *The Urantia Book*, purporting to have been edited by "an editorial staff of superhuman beings" and first published in 1955. The world according to Urantia is a dizzying array of universes populated by advanced beings of varying kinds, including "angels":

> Angels are the ministering-spirit associates of the evolutionary and ascending will creatures of all space; they are also the colleagues

DOCTOR LEONARD MCCOY

Once, just once, I'd like to be able to land somewhere and say, "Behold, I am the Archangel Gabriel."[2]

and working associates of the higher hosts of the divine personali-
ties of the spheres.... Together with the Messenger Hosts of Space,
the ministering spirits enjoy seasons of rest and change; they possess very social natures and have an associative capacity far tran-
scending that of human beings.[3]

Are Angels in Our Evolutionary Future?

Probably the most serious attempt to argue the angels-as-aliens
theory is Geddes MacGregor's book *Angels: Ministers of Grace*.
MacGregor notes that evolutionists regard "Lucy," a hominid dat-
ing from three million years ago, as our ancient ancestor. He points
out that modern man is markedly advanced physically and intel-
lectually in comparison to Lucy. He then suggests that angels might
be similarly advanced beings as far beyond us in the evolutionary
process as we are beyond Lucy.

> [Angels] could represent a further stage in the long evolutionary
> process of human development ... taking Lucy as a milestone along
> the road. If we are to take seriously the reality of the evolutionary
> process that is attested to by so many fields of modern scientific
> enquiry, the likelihood that beings exist who are intellectually and
> spiritually more advanced than we is surely overwhelming.[4]

For MacGregor, some such explanation of angels is the only
viable approach to salvaging their credibility today. The orthodox
view of angels as spiritual beings that God created as a separate
order of beings is, he opines, impossible to square with evolution.
We must, then, view angels as advanced beings from elsewhere in
the universe who evolved from beings like us who lived eons ago.
And if it happened out there, it might happen here: "If angels are to
be taken seriously today, they must represent a stage toward which
at least some human beings might be moving, however slowly, in
the course of a spiritual evolution."[5]

MORTIMER J. ADLER

[Angels] are not merely forms of extraterrestrial intelligence. They are
forms of extra-cosmic intelligence.[6]

Angels Are Aliens: Nonsense!

The theory that angels are really extraterrestrial beings from other planets is really nonsense. Two considerations make this conclusion essentially certain.

(1) The whole notion of aliens visiting Earth in spacecraft is a modern myth for which there is no real evidence — and indeed we have good reasons to dismiss it as false. The modern UFO craze began in the United States in the years immediately following World War II, when, coincidentally, the US government began experimenting with various kinds of powerful aircraft. For some reason the major UFO sightings and "crash scenes" were in the desert of the American Southwest — exactly where the military would be expected to be running its programs, but not the most likely places for aliens to be surveying.

As scientists have studied the parameters of Earth and the solar system that make biological life possible, it has become increasingly evident that such life must be extremely rare in the universe. And if intelligent beings do somehow live on other planets, it's even less likely that they would or even could make the journey here.[7]

(2) The biblical descriptions of angels simply don't fit the visitors-from-other-planets myth. For the theory to work, one must accept some of what the Bible says but throw out anything that doesn't fit. Perhaps most obviously, one must take the position that the little that angels do say in the Bible about themselves is a lie. Angels in the Bible claim to be messengers dispatched by the God who created the universe, not representatives of a planetary federation or of the community of space brothers.

Moreover, as we will see, the Bible presents angels as an entirely different order of being than humans or any other biological creatures. According to Scripture, angels are spirits, noncorporeal entities belonging to a realm of invisible realities. They are not visitors from elsewhere in the universe; they are rather visitors *to* our physical universe from a realm beyond the physical.

If we want to understand angels, then, we will have to look beyond the stars.

SENSE
Angels are powerful beings from beyond our world.

NONSENSE
Angels are superior beings from other planets.

Chapter 6

AN ANGEL'S A PERSON, NO MATTER HOW SMALL

Angels take traveling light to a whole new level.

If angels are not marvelously advanced beings from other planets, then what exactly are they? A seemingly obvious place to begin looking for the answer is with the word "angel" itself. As noted above, the word "angel" derives from the Greek word *angelos*, which is used in the Bible and which literally means "messenger." In fact, both the Hebrew word *mal'ak* and the Greek word *angelos* are occasionally used in the Bible to refer to human messengers. As the church father Augustine pointed out centuries ago, the word "angel" tells us something about what angels *do* but does not tell us what they *are*. The biblical word that best describes what angels are is the word "spirit." So, what are spirits?

Angels Are Spirits — but What Are Spirits?

Hebrews 1 twice refers to angels as "spirits" (Heb. 1:7, 14 NET). In one of those two occurrences, though, most modern translations render the word "winds" rather than "spirits": "Of the angels he says, 'He makes his angels winds, and his servants flames of fire'" (Heb. 1:7). You may be thinking that this is getting confusing, but it's not as complicated as it may seem.

In both the Hebrew language (the language in which the Old Testament was written) and the Greek language (used in ancient translations of the Old Testament and in the original New Testament), the word we translate "spirit" also means "wind" and "breath." The Hebrew word was *ruach*, and the Greek word was *pneuma* (from which we get the word "pneumatic," meaning something that uses moving air).

Thus, for example, the expression "the breath [*ruach* or *pneuma*] of life" refers to the capacity of animals and humans to breathe air as a necessary function of physical life (Gen. 6:17; 7:15). The words *ruach* and *pneuma* are also used to refer to "winds" that God caused to blow (Gen. 8:1). (In most places, though, where the Hebrew Old Testament uses *ruach* for "wind," the Greek translations use *anemos* instead of *pneuma*.)

The words *ruach* and *pneuma* have other uses of more obviously religious import. Most significantly, both are also used to describe what kind of being God is. For example, in the Old Testament we find this statement: "The Egyptians are human, and not God; their horses are flesh, and not spirit [*ruach*]" (Isa. 31:3). In Isaiah, the description of God as "spirit" is set in contrast to the description of the Egyptians' horses as "flesh."

This contrast between spirit and flesh is found frequently in the New Testament (e.g., Luke 24:39; John 3:6; Rom. 8:4–6; Gal. 6:8).[1] In some places human beings are described as being both flesh and spirit (1 Cor. 5:5; 2 Cor. 7:1) — that is, as having physical and nonphysical aspects. Likewise, when God is described as "spirit," the meaning is that God is a nonphysical being. Most famously, when Jesus said, "God is spirit [*pneuma*]," he was describing God as a nonphysical being who can therefore be worshiped at any location (John 4:20–24). So, in these and other ways, the Bible uses the word "spirit" to refer to nonphysical entities; this is its significance when used to refer to angelic beings.

AUGUSTINE

"Angel" is the name of their office, not of their nature.
If you seek the name of their nature, it is "spirit";
if you seek the name of their office, it is "angel":
from what they are, "spirit," from what they do, "angel."[2]

In Hebrews 1:7, the word *pneuma* is used in a quotation from Psalm 104:4, where there is a kind of play on words. The Hebrew text of Psalm 104:4 can be translated, "He makes the winds His messengers, flaming fire His ministers" (NASB). However, the verse can be read the other way around, and the words "messengers" (Heb. *mal²ak*) and "winds" (Heb. *ruach*) can also be translated "angels" and "spirits" respectively. Thus, in the Greek translation of the Old Testament (quoted in Heb. 1:7), the verse is rendered, "He makes his angels spirits and his ministers flames of fire." Both wind and fire are powerful forces that can move swiftly and are bodiless—and in fact the wind is invisible. Thus, angels are pictured in these verses as invisible beings who do not have bodies and who can move swiftly and powerfully in God's service.

Angels Have No Bodies but Are Not Nobodies

Most Christian theologians throughout history have understood the Bible to teach that angels are *incorporeal* beings—that is, beings who do not intrinsically possess bodies. (The word "body" means an object that occupies space and has at least a fairly stable structure and volume.) There is significant evidence to support this conclusion.

In addition to the reference to angels as spirits in Hebrews 1:7 and 14, the Bible frequently refers to demons as "spirits," usually in such expressions as "evil spirits" (1 Sam. 16:14–16, 23; 19:9; Matt. 12:43–45; Luke 7:21; 8:2; 11:24–26; Acts 19:12–16) or "unclean spirits" (e.g., Zech. 13:2; Matt. 10:1; Mark 1:23–27; Luke 4:36; Acts 5:16; Rev. 16:13).[3] These spirits are evidently incorporeal, since they can possess the bodies of human beings (see ch. 18). In the Gospels these evil and unclean spirits, or demons, are contrasted with the Holy Spirit (Matt. 12:22–32; Mark 3:22–30). The Holy Spirit is not said to "possess" people, but he can and does "fill" people in order to empower them to do God's will (e.g., Acts 6:3, 5; Eph. 5:18).

HEBREWS 1:14

Are not all angels spirits in the divine service,
    sent out to serve for the sake of those who are to inherit salvation?

These and other actions of the Holy Spirit are most easily (and are widely) understood to imply that he also does not have a body.

Another thing angels can do that implies they are incorporeal is to appear to people in their dreams (e.g., Matt. 1:20, 24; 2:13, 19). Matthew is not saying here that Joseph had a dream about an angel; he says that an angel of the Lord actually appeared to Joseph in his dreams. This is best explained on the assumption that angels don't have bodies.

Some readers of the Bible have mistakenly thought that Paul was referring to angels when he talked about "celestial" or "heavenly" bodies (1 Cor. 15:40). But Paul tells us in the very next breath what bodies he has in mind: the sun, moon, and stars are the heavenly bodies (v. 41), not angels (which are never mentioned in the entire chapter).

Angels, then, do not have bodies. This has some interesting implications for certain popular notions about angels, which we will examine in the next chapter.

SENSE

Angels are spirits.

NONSENSE

Spirits have bodies.

Chapter 7

OF MEN, WOMEN, AND ANGELS

Angels can appear in bodily form, but they don't come in male and female varieties.

In the previous chapter, we gave reasons for thinking (as most Christians have thought) that angels are incorporeal beings. You may be wondering, though, about those passages in the Bible in which angels were visible to human eyes—and at least seemed to have bodies.

They Saw Some Body

Indeed angels could appear in bodily form. The biblical evidence shows that on such occasions the angels were given physical form *temporarily*. That is, physical embodiment was not their normal mode of existence. Angels belong by nature to the realm of the "invisible" creation in contrast to the "visible" world we see around us (cf. Col. 1:16).

In biblical accounts of their visits to human beings, angels generally seem to appear suddenly and then disappear without any explanation. For example, when the women discovered Jesus' tomb to be empty and the stone rolled away, Luke tells us, "Suddenly, two men in dazzling clothes stood beside them," causing the women to fall on the ground in terror (Luke 24:4–5). (John refers to these two individuals as "angels" in John 20:12; see also Luke 24:22–23.)

So, when angels did appear, their physical forms were evidently temporary ones taken for the purpose of interacting with human beings and not their own intrinsic forms.

Since angels do not intrinsically have physical bodies, certain facts about them follow—facts that will help us recognize a lot of contemporary angel lore as unreliable.

Guess Who's Coming to Dinner?[1]

If angels are not physical beings, it follows that they do not need to eat. Only if they assume physical bodies like ours will they even have the capacity to eat.

Angels are mentioned as having eaten only twice in the entire Bible—and on the same day. In Genesis 18 "the LORD" appeared to Abraham (Gen. 18:1). The text then says immediately that Abraham saw "three men" and offered to feed them and wash their feet (18:2–5). Abraham and his wife Sarah then hurriedly prepared a meal, and "they ate" (18:8). (We aren't told if Abraham actually washed their feet, though presumably he did.)

Then "the LORD" spoke at some length with Abraham, while "the men" (presumably the two who had accompanied the Lord) left to go down to Sodom (Gen. 18:22). Later we are told that these were "two angels" or "two messengers" (19:1) and that when they went to Sodom that same evening, they stayed with Abraham's nephew Lot, who also offered to wash their feet and served them a meal (19:2–3). The next day "the angels" took Lot and his family out of Sodom to avoid being destroyed with the rest of the town (19:15–16).[2] They agreed to spare one of the smaller towns in the plain (called Zoar) so that Lot could take his family there (19:17–22).

These two angels—assuming they were actual spiritual, angelic beings—are the only angels said to have eaten anywhere in the Bible. Elsewhere in the Bible, spiritual beings do not eat physical food when presented with the opportunity. When the "angel of the LORD" is offered food by hospitable people in the book of Judges, he does not eat it but instead has it "consumed" by fire in a burnt offering (Judg. 6:18–22; 13:15–20). (We will discuss the identity of this mysterious "angel of the LORD" in ch. 10.) After Jesus rose from the dead, to prove to his disciples that he was not a mere "spirit," he ate a piece of broiled fish in front of them (Luke 24:36–43). These incidents don't prove that angels *can't* eat, but they suggest that for any spirits to eat is at least abnormal.

There are three possible interpretations that make sense of all the information we have. (1) One might surmise that the two visitors who accompanied the Lord when he met Abraham and who then went to visit Lot were actually human beings, not angelic beings. The Hebrew word *mal'ak*, which we translate "angel," literally means "messenger" — and doesn't necessarily refer to the spiritual beings God created to serve as his messengers.

Although nothing in Genesis absolutely precludes the idea that the visitors were human beings,[3] the general sense that almost everyone has when reading the text is that these "messengers" came from heaven with God. They show up with the Lord, speak on his behalf to Lot, blind the men of Sodom who threaten Lot, are authorized to spare one of the towns from the Lord's judgment at Lot's request, and disappear from the narrative after their task with Lot is done. All of these actions are possible for human beings, but cumulatively the best explanation is that when the text refers to them as "angels" this means spiritual, heavenly beings.[4]

(2) One might infer that the angels only *appeared* to eat. Ancient Jewish interpretations of the passage consistently took this approach. The first-century Jewish philosopher Philo wrote, "It is a marvel indeed that though they neither ate nor drank, they gave the appearance of both eating and drinking." Likewise, the late first-century Jewish historian Josephus stated that the angels "gave to him the appearance of having consumed."[5] The main objection to this traditional interpretation — which should not be lightly dismissed — is that Genesis says the men "ate" (Gen. 18:8; 19:3), with no indication that this is mere appearance.

(3) This leaves us with a third possible explanation: the angels really ate the food, but were able to do so only because they had temporarily taken human form. The angels ate the food offered to

them by Abraham and Lot, not because they needed to eat but in order to honor the hospitality that Abraham and Lot were showing them. That hospitality stands in stark contrast to the inhospitable conduct of the people of Sodom (Gen. 19:4–9).

The lack of care for the poor and needy—characteristically demonstrated in the ancient world through hospitality—was one of the grievous sins, along with sexual perversion, of Sodom and Gomorrah (Ezek. 16:49; see also Isa. 1:9–10, 17).[6] In this context, the angels may have taken ordinary human form and eaten food in order to give Abraham and Lot an opportunity to show their true character before delivering to them their good news (that Abraham would have a son in his old age, and that Lot was to be spared the judgment on the cities in the plain).

Some Christians think that angels regularly eat in heaven. In support of this idea, they quote a reference to "the bread of angels" (Ps. 78:25).[7] Let's look at this passage:

> He rained manna for them to eat;
> He gave them grain from heaven.
> People ate the bread of angels;[8]
> He sent them an abundant supply of food. (Ps. 78:24–25 HCSB)

After the Israelites had escaped from Egypt, God had provided for them a breadlike food that covered the ground in the morning. The Israelites, who had never seen it before, called the bread *manna*, which meant "what is it?" (Ex. 16:14–15, 31). This wasn't literally angel food, nor was it literally delivered from heavenly pantry shelves down to the wilderness!

The psalmist, then, is using the expression "bread of angels" figuratively, to describe the bread as a marvelous provision from God. He is not saying that angels literally eat bread, or even that angels literally eat anything in heaven. As incorporeal spirits, angels don't need to eat anything.

Sorry, Angels Are Not "Babes"

If angels are incorporeal, it also follows that they do not have gender. Maleness and femaleness are biologically based distinctions that simply have no relevance to beings who do not possess bodies. This applies not only to angels but also to God, who is not literally a male. Although the Bible normally speaks of God using male imagery (e.g., "Father," "King") and pronouns ("he"), God is by nature neither male nor female, but an incorporeal, infinite Spirit (John 4:24).[9]

Likewise, angels are neither male nor female beings. Throughout the Bible, angels are referred to using masculine pronouns and are sometimes called "men," but no description is ever given that indicates that they are literally male. The Bible uses masculine language for angels because that is the "default" way of speaking when the gender of the individual is unknown or irrelevant. And the Bible *never* speaks of any angels as feminine or female in nature.

It is interesting to note that many contemporary angel stories include overt descriptions of the supposed angels as male or female. The first angel described by John Randolph Price in his book *The Angels within Us* has "the face and form of a beautiful woman wearing a flowing white robe trimmed in gold."[10] Stories of very masculine angels are also told. In one such story, a woman saw an angel who "looked like a clean-cut, boy-next-door football player ... only larger and very muscular."[11] Perhaps we should not be surprised that women often see the handsome male angels, while men often see the beautiful female angels!

Although we know of no biblical reason why angels *could not* appear in overtly masculine or feminine forms, the modern detailed descriptions of angels have no precedent in Scripture. For the most part, biblical angels are nondescript.[12] The most specific description of any angel's human appearance in the Bible is that of "a young man" (Mark 16:5).[13] We must therefore be cautious in listening to modern descriptions of angelic appearances.

The more detail we are given about their gender, attractiveness, hair color, clothing, and so forth, the more likely it is that the person isn't a literal angel at all. Perhaps most troubling are descriptions of angels as sensuous beings, whether ruggedly handsome males or softly beautiful females. Such descriptions are dead giveaways that the "angels" are either fictions of imagination, human beings misidentified as angels, or even possibly demonic appearances.

SENSE

Angels can appear in human form.

NONSENSE

Angels are overtly male or female beings.

Chapter 8

WE'RE NO ANGELS

Humans were not in heaven before birth, and we won't become angels after death.

If angels don't have bodies and don't come in male and female genders, as we argued in the previous two chapters, then some other popular notions about angels may also have to be reconsidered. Among them is the idea that human beings either *used to be* angels before "coming" to Earth or *will become* angels after death. These ideas, which have been around for a long time, have gotten considerable popular exposure in numerous films and television programs.

We Were Not Angels before Our Births

In the 1940 film *The Blue Bird*, Shirley Temple plays a little girl who visits heaven and encounters a large group of children waiting their turn to be born. As a whimsical fantasy, such a story can be both entertaining and moving—but it's not good theology.

Biblically speaking, human beings do not preexist as heavenly or spiritual beings prior to their physical, earthly lives. The very first human being, Adam, became a "living being" when God formed his body from the ground and breathed life into him (Gen. 2:7). The picture here is not of a personal soul being sent into a human body, but of life being imparted to a human body. In the New Testament, the apostle Paul states that Adam originated from the earth, in contrast to Jesus Christ, who *did* originate from heaven (1 Cor. 15:47).

Jesus, in fact, is the only human being whose existence as a person predated his human life on earth. Note the contrast that is made in the following passage between John the Baptist, as one who "is from the earth," and Jesus, who "comes from heaven" and "is above all": "The one who comes from above is above all; the one who is of the earth belongs to the earth and speaks about earthly things. The one who comes from heaven is above all" (John 3:31).

The fact that human beings begin to exist at their physical conception, not in a preexistent life in heaven, completely undermines certain deviant forms of Christianity. For example, Mormonism teaches that all human beings existed as male and female spirit children of God in heaven before coming to the earth. This key element of their doctrinal system, as unobjectionable as it may seem to many in our culture, is at odds with the biblical view of humanity.

We Will Not Become Angels

Perhaps even more common today is the notion that human beings become angels after they die. In popular angel mythology, human beings die and then come back to the earth as angels, either to help those they left behind or others in similar difficulties.

According to the Bible, angels are a class of beings who existed before any humans had ever died. We know this because some of those angelic beings rebelled against God, and their leader, the Devil, tempted Eve (Gen. 3).

Moreover, the Bible makes it clear that departed human spirits, unlike angels, are generally not permitted to visit or communicate with human beings. In Jesus' parable of Lazarus and the rich man, for example, the rich man's request for someone to visit his brothers and warn them of the judgment to come was turned down (Luke 16:19–31). The Old Testament forbids communication with the dead (Lev. 19:31; Deut. 18:11; Isa. 8:19).

On one occasion a departed human spirit was apparently enabled to communicate with living human beings. The biblical account, however, proves the general point being made here. Saul, the Israelite king, asked a medium to conjure the deceased prophet

Samuel, and evidently Samuel did appear (1 Sam. 28:3–20). The medium's astonishment at seeing Samuel (v. 12) shows that her conjuring had nothing to do with Samuel's arrival and that normally such visitations did not happen (at least to her!). We may also note that the passage does not identify the departed spirit of Samuel as an angel.

The New Testament makes it clear that human beings following their death are in a spiritual state separated from the living and are awaiting their resurrection from the dead. The resurrection will be a future event in which the dead are restored to life as physically embodied, human beings (John 5:28–29; Acts 24:15). For those who are right with God, this resurrection will consummate their redemption with glorified, immortal, incorruptible bodies ready for eternal life (Rom. 8:23; 1 Cor. 15:42–57). Thus, God's plan for human beings after they die is not to become angels, but to await resurrection to immortal, eternal life as glorified, perfected human beings.

In the sense that we will possess immortality, it is true that in the resurrection we will become *like* the angels. Jesus once commented on this very point. Earlier in this book (ch. 4) we mentioned that on one occasion some Sadducees debated Jesus on the matter of a future resurrection, which they did not accept. Their objection involved a far-fetched story of a woman marrying seven brothers in turn as each one died and left her a childless widow. The Sadducees suggested that such a scenario would pose a problem in the resurrection, because then she would have to be recognized as the wife of all seven men (Luke 20:27–33). Here was Jesus' response:

> The sons of this age marry and are given in marriage. But those who are counted worthy to take part in that age and in the resurrection from the dead neither marry nor are given in marriage. For they cannot die anymore, because they are like angels and are sons of God, since they are sons of the resurrection. (Luke 20:34–36 HCSB).

We must be careful not to read too much into Jesus' comments here. What Jesus says explicitly is that angels do not get married and they do not die. The more general point that Jesus is making here is that angels don't have a life cycle like ours of birth, marriage, procreation, and death. The hypothetical seven-time widow won't be going back into such a life cycle in the resurrection, but will instead be part of a new world of immortal human beings. What Jesus does not say is that human beings will become angels. Rather, he says that they will become *like* angels, in the way that he specifies.[1]

There is some really good news here. On the one hand, it appears that everything good that angels have that we presently do not have will be ours in the resurrection. We will be immortal, perfect creatures. We will have direct, unfettered access to God. We will no doubt have power and knowledge beyond anything we can experience in our present mortal, fallen condition.

> We will have the best of both worlds.

On the other hand, we will retain certain aspects of human nature that most of us consider quite wonderful. We will enjoy being part of nature, the physical world in which we were created. Although we will not need to perpetuate the species through the procreative cycle, there is every reason to think we will retain our gender distinctions as men and women—just as Jesus, who rose from the dead to become the source of resurrection life for us, is still a male human being (Acts 17:31). It would not be going too far to say that we will have the best of both worlds; that is just as God intended.

SENSE
We will be immortal, like the angels, in the resurrection.

NONSENSE
We were angels before our births or will become angels after we die.

Chapter 9

ANGELS CAN'T HOLD A CANDLE TO GOD

The most important thing you can know about angels is that they're not divine.

Angels are fascinating creatures. Their supernatural nature and power, their pivotal roles in some of the Bible's most notable events, and the sheer mystery that faces us as we try to think about them give angels enormous appeal.

Why, then, would anyone be troubled by all the attention that angels are getting today? One reason—and it's something that no doubt troubles the angels themselves—people are looking to angels in ways that they should be looking only to God.

Putting Angels in God's Place

As an example of fascination with angels run amok, consider what Karen Goldman says in her book *Angel Encounters* about her own experiences with angels. Goldman tells us that she fell in love with angels and that they "made all the difference" in her life, bringing her out of "a period of terrible darkness." She learned to "trust" them and received assurance that her life would work out beautifully. She knew as a result of her encounters with angels that she was "deeply loved" and "infinitely befriended." "The angels have been very gracious," she testifies. "My heart is alive now, because it knows it has angels."[1]

Goldman is speaking about angels the way that she should be speaking about God. It is God whom we all need to trust, from whom we need to receive grace, in whom alone we can find infinite love, and who alone can bring us out of our spiritual darkness and make our hearts truly alive.

The angels would be first in line to rebuke anyone who looks to them with such reverence and hope. When the apostle John started to fall before an angel to worship him, the angel said, "Do not do it! I am a fellow servant with you and with your brothers who hold to the testimony of Jesus. Worship God!" (Rev. 19:10 NIV; see also 22:8–9).

Putting Angels in Their Place

Some anonymous wag[2] once observed that there were two fundamental laws of reality:

> There is a God.
> You are not Him.

Perhaps we should add, "And neither are angels." They are, like us, fundamentally *creatures*. The Bible numbers the angels among God's created works, along with the physical universe (Neh. 9:6; Pss. 103:19–22; 148:2–5). They are God's "servants," "ministering spirits" whom God dispatches to do his will (Heb. 1:7, 14). As

---
If you think angels are wonderful, you should get to know God!

---

we have seen, they do not want to be worshiped, nor should they be (see also Col. 2:18).

Most writers on angels acknowledge that angels are not God. Yet they too often confuse angels with God by attributing powers or characteristics to them that belong only to God. Even some people who generally accept a Christian perspective on angels fall into such error. One writer states, "Angels are capable of seeing the past, the present, and the future all at once."[3] This is news to us! The Bible attributes such knowledge to God alone.

Unfortunately, there is a long history in Christianity of looking to angels in spiritually unhealthy ways. Many theologians and church leaders, while being careful to say that Christians should not worship angels, have encouraged a religious devotion to angels that is nevertheless excessive. Catholic theology distinguishes between worship, which believers may offer to God alone, and veneration, which they may offer to Mary, the saints, and the angels. This distinction allows Catholics to pursue close spiritual relationships with angels, to pray to angels, to build shrines to angels, and to express ardent love, thanks, and honor to angels. None of this has any precedent in the Bible, which limits prayer and other expressions of religious devotion to God. We will come back to this point in chapter 15.

Worse still, some people view angels with more enthusiasm and show more devotion to angels than they do toward God. Before Karen Goldman discovered angels, she didn't care much for God.

> Is God laughing at us? Are we absolutely meaningless? Is this all a big horrific, sadistic joke?... I didn't like being around people, I didn't like life or myself and certainly not God.... I felt God owed me a miracle or, at least, I knew I needed one. But even when I prayed it was to a God I no longer trusted.[4]

Sadly, the God whom she professed to find through the angels is not the Creator and Lord spoken of in the Bible. Even before she "found angels," Goldman was heavily involved in the New Age movement. She worked for the Sedona Institute, a major New Age center that taught her a spiritual practice called "releasing," which she eventually used to write about angels.[5]

The "God" that Goldman extols is essentially a pantheistic concept. Pantheism teaches that everything is God—and therefore we ourselves are God, or parts of God. As Goldman puts it, "The angels are ever within and around us, just as we are ever within and a part of God.... We are not in a master/slave bond with the Divine but in an integral union. We are as much a part of It as It is of us. We are all made of the same stuff, each of us a slice of the infinite pie."[6]

The Bible emphatically rejects pantheism. "In the beginning God created the heavens and the earth" (Gen. 1:1 NIV). "Know that the LORD is God. *It is he that made us, and we are his; we are his people, and the sheep of his pasture*" (Ps. 100:3). "They exchanged the truth about God for a lie and worshiped and served the creature rather than the Creator, who is blessed forever! Amen" (Rom. 1:25).

Putting angels in their place, then, is just part of the all-important necessity of *putting ourselves in our place*. If we think of angels as divine, it will become a lot easier to think of ourselves as divine, too — and in fact the two typically go hand in hand. By contrast, if we recognize that angels, however wonderful, are not divine but (in comparison to God) lowly servants and creatures, we will more clearly recognize that we, too, are God's creatures.

If you think angels are wonderful, you should get to know God! After all, he made them. Perhaps a lot of the obsession in our culture over angels is due to the fact that people view God as distant, unapproachable, or uncaring. But we have good news: God really is infinitely loving, gracious, and good, and he has done something quite extraordinary to address our need. We find the story of what God has done for us in the Bible. As we continue our study of angels in the rest of this book, we're going to hit on some of the highlights of that story. It is the story that the angels most want you to hear.

SENSE

Angels are among God's most wonderful creatures.

NONSENSE

Angels are divine beings or ways of experiencing God.

Chapter 10

WHEN IS AN ANGEL NOT AN ANGEL?

When he's the angel of the LORD, the Mystery Man of the Old Testament.

The most mysterious figure in the Bible, arguably, is "the angel of the LORD," a figure who is seen several times in Genesis and who shows up in various places throughout the rest of the Old Testament. He is called "the angel of the LORD" (lit., "the angel of Yahweh" or "the angel of Jehovah") and "the angel of God," but this angel is also called "the LORD," "God," simply "angel," and even "a man." So, who was he? *What* was he?

Keep in mind that the biblical words we translate "angel" (Heb. *mal'ak*; Gk. *angelos*) mean "messenger." They don't necessarily refer to the spiritual beings whom God created and who often serve as his messengers. Whenever you see the expression "the angel of the LORD," you can remind yourself that this could also be translated "the messenger of the LORD." There are good reasons to think that this person was not literally what we would call an "angel" at all.

Did I Just See God?

The first time "the angel of the LORD" is mentioned is in one of the lesser-known passages in Genesis. Abram and Sarai (as they were known before being called Abraham and Sarah) were still childless,

56

and Sarai had arranged for Abram to father a child by her maid, Hagar. Predictably, after Hagar became pregnant, Sarai became jealous of Hagar and mistreated her to the point that Hagar ran away into the wilderness (Gen. 16:1–6). There "the angel of the LORD" spoke to her, telling her to return to her mistress.

But then he says something odd, coming from an angel: "I will so greatly multiply your offspring that they cannot be counted for multitude" (Gen. 16:10). One would expect God to say this, not an angel, and indeed later God tells Abraham essentially the same thing about the descendants of Hagar's son Ishmael (17:20). In his next words to Hagar, the "angel" speaks about "the LORD" in the third person: "The LORD has given heed to your affliction" (16:11). But then we are told that Hagar "named of the LORD who spoke to her, 'You are El-roi' [a God who sees]; for she said, 'Have I really seen God and remained alive after seeing him?'" (16:13). So was it the Lord who spoke to her, or an angel representing the Lord?

This pattern of apparent inconsistency is repeated (consistently!) in later incidents involving "the angel of the LORD." After Hagar's son Ishmael was born and the two of them were forced to leave, "the angel of God called to Hagar from heaven," speaking *about* God—"*God* has heard the voice of the boy"—and also speaking as if he *were* God—"*I* will make a great nation of him" (Gen. 21:17–18). When Abraham went up the mountain years later to sacrifice Isaac, "the angel of the LORD called to him from heaven" and told him, "Now I know that you fear *God*, since you have not withheld your son, your only son, from *me*" (22:11–12).

Similarly, Abraham's grandson Jacob reported a dream in which "the angel of God" spoke to him with the words, "I am the God of Bethel" (Gen. 31:11, 13). In one of the stranger events recorded in Genesis, Jacob later wrestled with "a man" all night who refused to tell Jacob his name; when it was over, Jacob named the spot Peniel (which means "face of God"), commenting, "I have seen God face to face" (32:24–30). When Jacob (renamed Israel) spoke blessings on his grandchildren Ephraim and Manasseh, he spoke of an "angel" as if he were God:

> *The God* before whom my ancestors Abraham and Isaac walked,
> *The God* who has been my shepherd all my life to this day,
> *The angel* who has redeemed me from all evil,
> Bless the boys. (Gen. 48:15–16)

This enigmatic figure shows up again in Exodus. In Moses' famous encounter with God in the burning bush, it was "the angel of the LORD" who appeared to him from the bush, but what he said was spoken as if he were God: "I am the God of your father.... I have observed the misery of my people who are in Egypt.... I have come down to deliver them" (Ex. 3:1–8). When Moses led the Israelites out of Egypt, "the LORD went in front of them in a pillar of cloud by day ... and in a pillar of fire by night" (13:21). This manifestation of God in association with the pillar of cloud and fire is called both "the angel of God" and "the LORD" (14:19, 24). After the Israelites reached Mount Sinai and had been given the Law (including the Ten Commandments), God told them:

> See, I am sending an angel ahead of you.... Do not rebel against him; he will not forgive your rebellion, since *my Name is in him*. If you listen carefully to what *he* says and do all that *I* say, I will be an enemy to your enemies.... Worship the LORD your God, and his blessing will be on your food and water. *I* will take away sickness from among you. (Ex. 23:20–25 NIV)

We find this pattern repeated in later books of the Old Testament as well, especially in Judges, where this shadowy figure is called "the LORD" or "God," "the angel of the LORD" or "of God," and "a man of God" (Judg. 2:1–4; 6:11–27; 13:3–22).

Perhaps most startling are the references to the angel of the Lord in Zechariah, one of the last books of the Old Testament. In that book, the angel of the Lord talks *to* the Lord: "Then the angel of the LORD said, 'O LORD of hosts ...'" (Zech. 1:12). Further on in the same book, the angel of the Lord again seems to speak as if he *is* the Lord, this time calling on the Lord to rebuke the devil!

> Then he showed me the high priest Joshua standing before the angel of the LORD, and Satan standing at his right hand to accuse him. And the LORD said to Satan, "The LORD rebuke you, O Satan! The LORD who has chosen Jerusalem rebuke you!" (Zech. 3:1–2)

Identifying the Mystery Man

Some critics of the Bible suggest that these passages are composite texts in which two different versions of the same story have been woven together. In one version, the visitor was the Lord; in another version, the visitor was the Lord's angel; and the resulting text confuses the two figures. The "interchangeability" of the angel of the Lord with the Lord himself, however, "cannot be resolved by assuming a clumsy merging of two traditional stories."[1] This is because repeatedly in Genesis, Exodus, and Judges, and occasionally in other books such as Zechariah, the same pattern emerges, however enigmatic it may seem.

A more credible view is that the Old Testament sometimes speaks of the angel of the Lord as if he were the Lord because he was acting as his representative. Some evangelical scholars endorse this interpretation. Ben Witherington explains:

> The angel of the Lord is just that—an angel. The angel of the Lord is a special representative or messenger of God to God's people, and according to the ancient concept of agency, he could be considered to be the Lord who sent them, and was to be treated as if he were the one who sent him.[2]

This opinion can explain some of what we find in the biblical texts, but not everything. For example, although human beings cannot see God and live (Ex. 33:20), when people see the angel of the Lord they frequently say with surprise that they have seen God and yet lived (Gen. 16:13; 32:30; Judg. 6:22–23; 13:22). The agency view implies that these people were all mistaken (something never suggested in the texts). Jacob credits "the angel" with redeeming him from all evil (Gen. 48:15–16). Zechariah speaks of the angel of the Lord as if he were the Lord, even when the "angel" is speaking *to the Lord*—not just when he is speaking to human beings on God's behalf. If the agency view were correct, we would expect the Old Testament prophets, who were also God's agents, to speak (at least occasionally) as if they were God. They do not. Instead, they routinely introduce God's word by saying things like, "Thus says the LORD." Somehow, this mysterious "angel" both *is* the Lord and is distinguished *from* the Lord as his messenger.

The identity of this divine figure is revealed in the New Testament: He is the person known in his human life as Jesus Christ. Christians as early as the second century (such as Justin Martyr) have explicitly recognized the angel of the Lord as a preincarnate manifestation of the Lord Jesus.[3] Like the angel of the Lord, Christ is spoken of as being God and also as being distinct from and sent from God. John calls him "the Word" (Gk. *logos*) and opens his gospel with this statement: "In the beginning was the Word, and the Word was *with God*, and the Word *was God*" (John 1:1).

Some religious groups, finding the above statement contradictory or confusing, have tried to make John's theology easier to grasp by "fixing" the translation. The Jehovah's Witnesses, for example, in their New World Translation, render the last line, "and the Word was *a god*." But John was no more confused than were the Old Testament writers who wrote about the angel of the Lord. Jesus was and is in some mysterious way God and also distinct from God. "No one has ever seen God. It is God the only Son, who is close to the Father's heart, who has made him known" (John 1:18).

Biblical scholar Duane Garrett has pointed out something else in the New Testament that fits with identifying the mysterious angel of the Lord with Jesus Christ. The New Testament uses the term "angel of the Lord" several times (Matt. 1:20, 24; 2:13, 19; 28:2; Luke 1:11; 2:9; Acts 5:19; 8:26; 12:7, 23). However, Garrett notices that none of these references to an "angel of the Lord" speaks of him in any way suggestive of deity; the angel in these passages never speaks of himself as God.

> If it was legitimate for an angel to do this in the Old Testament, why not in the New Testament? To me, the most reasonable explanation is that in the Old Testament, the Logos alone, and not the angels, took on the identity of God. After the Logos became incarnate as Jesus Christ, any appearance He made would not be in the form of an angel but as the risen Christ.[4]

So then, it appears that the angel of the Lord in the Old Testament was actually the Son of God, coming to earth in visible form before he became the physical, human being known as Jesus. Those mysterious encounters with the angel of the Lord were precursors to Christ's coming—anticipating the day when God would take human form.

SENSE

The angel of the LORD was Jesus before he came to the earth as a man.

NONSENSE

The angel of the Lord was just an angel speaking for God.

Chapter 11

JESUS IS COMING— OR IS THAT MICHAEL?

Jesus Christ is not the chief angel, but the One whom the angels worship.

As we saw in the previous chapter, the "angel of the LORD" was not a created angel but was the Lord God himself. In the New Testament he is identified as Jesus Christ. However, some religious groups—most notably the Jehovah's Witnesses—think that Jesus wasn't really God but was rather the greatest angelic spirit, created by God to rule over the rest of his creation. Specifically, they teach that Jesus was Michael the archangel. Is that true?

No. There are two simple reasons why Jesus cannot be identified as Michael the archangel: Michael is a lesser figure than Jesus, and Jesus is much more than an archangel.

Michael Is Not Jesus

The angel Michael is mentioned only five times in the Bible. He is introduced in Daniel 10:13, where another angel tells Daniel that "Michael, one of the chief princes," helped him in a conflict with "the prince of the kingdom of Persia." The description "one of the chief princes" makes it clear that although Michael was an angel of high rank, he did not have an exclusive position as the ruler of all the angels. The angel went on to refer to Michael as "your prince," meaning the prince of Israel (10:21). Thus, toward the end of the book Daniel is told, "Now at that time Michael, the great prince, the protector of your people, shall arise" (12:1). Michael, then, was an angel specially assigned to protect Israel from spiritual attack.

In the epistle of Jude we read: "But Michael the archangel, when he disputed with the devil and argued about the body of Moses, did not dare pronounce against him a railing judgment, but said, 'The Lord rebuke you!'" (Jude 9 NASB). Michael's reticence to speak a word of judgment against the Devil implies that Michael was not the Devil's superior. But Jesus clearly was and is the Devil's superior (e.g., Matt. 28:19; Eph. 1:20–21; Col. 1:16–17).

In one of John's visions in the book of Revelation, "Michael and his angels" battled "the dragon [the Devil] and his angels," with the result that the dragon and his angels were cast out of heaven down to the earth (Rev. 12:7–9). Some people have thought that Michael's role in battling the Devil shows that he is really Jesus. However, in this vision Jesus is represented as "a son, a male child, who is to rule all the nations with a rod of iron" (v. 5). Michael's role here is essentially the same as in Daniel: he fights the spiritual forces that threaten God's people.

Jesus: More than an Archangel

Those who contend that Jesus is an archangel often quote 1 Thessalonians 4:16: "For the Lord himself will come down from heaven, with a loud command, with the voice of the archangel and with the trumpet call of God" (NIV). But this is an odd statement if Jesus *is* an archangel. With what other kind of voice would he speak? Paul does not mean that Jesus will speak with his own archangelic voice, but that when Jesus returns an archangel's cry will herald his descent.

The main reason why Michael and Jesus cannot be the same person is that Jesus is far more than an archangel; he is God.[1] The book of Hebrews affirms in no uncertain terms that Jesus is God's Son, the Lord whom all the angels worship (Heb. 1:4–6), not one of the angels. Indeed, the Bible never calls Jesus "Michael," but it does call Jesus "God" several times (Isa. 9:6; John 1:1, 18; 20:28; Acts 20:28; Rom. 9:5; Titus 2:13; Heb. 1:8; 2 Peter 1:1). Yet some people insist that Jesus is Michael but not God!

The New Testament teaches us to think of Jesus as God in a variety of ways beyond simply calling him "God." It also calls Jesus "Lord" in contexts where this title stands for the divine name Yahweh (or Jehovah), translated "LORD" in the Old Testament. For example, in Romans 10:9–12 the apostle Paul says that whoever confesses that Jesus is "Lord" will be saved because he is the same "Lord" for both Jews and non-Jews, richly able to save everyone who calls on him. Paul then supports his point with a quotation from Joel 2:32: "For, 'everyone who calls on the name of the Lord will be saved'" (Rom. 10:13 NIV). But in the Hebrew text of Joel 2:32 it is "the name of Yahweh" on which people are to call to be saved. The New Testament calls Jesus "Lord" in this way several times (e.g., Phil. 2:9–11 [see Isa. 45:23]; 1 Peter 2:3–8 [see Ps. 34:8]; 1 Peter 3:14–15 [see Isa. 8:12–13]).

> The Bible never calls Jesus "Michael," but it does call Jesus "God" several times. Yet some people insist that Jesus is Michael but not God!

The New Testament applies other divine titles to Jesus. These include titles found elsewhere only of God, such as "the first and the last" (Rev. 1:17; 22:13; cf. Isa. 44:6) and "King of kings and Lord of lords" (Rev. 17:14; 19:16; cf. 1 Tim. 6:15). Jesus also receives titles that in their ultimate, spiritual sense belong only to God and are used of Jesus in the same way. For example, Jesus is the Savior (Luke 2:11; John 4:42; Titus 2:13; 1 John 4:14; cf. Isa. 43:11; 45:21–22; 1 Tim. 4:10), the Shepherd (John 10:11; Heb. 13:20; cf. Ps. 23:1; Isa. 40:11), and the Rock (1 Cor. 10:4; cf. Isa. 44:8).

Jesus also has characteristics or attributes that mark him as God. We are told that Jesus has God's very nature (Phil. 2:6; Col. 2:9; Heb. 1:3). Like God, he is eternal, without beginning or ending of existence (John 1:1; 8:58; 17:5; Col. 1:17; Heb. 1:2; 7:3). Like God, he is omnipresent, or existing everywhere simultaneously (Matt. 18:20; 28:20; John 3:13; Eph. 1:23; 4:10; Col. 3:11). Like God, he is omniscient or all-knowing (John 16:30) and unchangeable in his essence (Heb. 1:11–12).

God is as God does, one might say, and Jesus does what God does. In fact, on one occasion Jesus claimed that as the Son he could do *only* what the Father did, and that he did *whatever* the Father did *in the same way* that the Father did it (John 5:19). The New Testament teaches that Jesus the Son did the work of creation (Heb. 1:10). Paul says that everything was made in, through, and for him, and that he holds the universe together (Col. 1:16; see also Heb. 1:3). Jesus also claimed God's prerogative to forgive sins (Mark 2:1–12) and to judge the world (Matt. 25:31–46; John 5:20–30).

From a practical vantage point, the New Testament also teaches us to approach or treat Jesus as God. Thus, we are told to "honor the Son just as [we] honor the Father" (John 5:23). We are encouraged to pray to Jesus (John 14:14; 1 Cor. 1:2; 2 Cor. 12:8–10), to worship Jesus as the angels themselves do (Matt. 28:17; Heb. 1:6), to trust in Jesus as we trust in God (John 14:1), and to give him the praise and glory due to God (2 Tim. 4:18; 2 Peter 3:18; Rev. 5:13).

Jesus and Michael: Not the Same

All in all, the Bible's portrayal of Jesus Christ clearly differentiates him from Michael. In fairness, some Christians in the past have identified Jesus as Michael in a way that does not deny that Jesus is God. They have held that Michael was simply one of the names of the preincarnate Son of God. They have further suggested that the title "archangel" does not classify Michael *as* an angel but rather means that he is the ruler *over* all the angels. This theory, while it avoids demoting Jesus from God to creature, is almost certainly wrong. As we have seen, Michael is described in the book of Daniel as "one of the chief princes" (Dan. 10:13), that is, one of a number of beings who are just like him.

Moreover, the form of the word "archangel" means a chief or ruling angel,[2] and the title "archangel" in Jewish usage was customarily understood as referring to a ruling angel. In fact, the title was applicable to several angelic beings. Nothing in the Bible limits the title "archangel" to Michael alone. Jude 9 calls him "Michael the archangel," but the word "the" here does not make Michael the only archangel. (To understand why it doesn't, compare such biblical expressions as "Isaiah the prophet" or "the angel Gabriel.")[3] It is best, then, to reject this theory. Michael is a leader among the angels, not the Lord of the angels.

SENSE

Michael is one of the most powerful and important angels.

NONSENSE

Michael is another name for Jesus.

Chapter 12

NAME THAT ANGEL, OR, PIN THE WING ON THE SERAPH

Angels have many names and do different things, but we don't know how they are ranked.

Four centuries or so after Paul proclaimed and defended the gospel to the cultured and intellectual people of Athens, an unknown writer composed several books in the name of Dionysius, one of Paul's Athenian converts (Acts 17:34). Dionysius was an "Areopagite"—a member of the Areopagus council, a kind of city board of governors named for the hill where they sometimes met. The pseudonym Dionysius (or Denis, as his name is sometimes anglicized) was generally accepted as the name of the books' true author until modern times.

One of these books by Pseudo-Dionysius, as modern scholars call him, was a work on angels entitled *Celestial Hierarchy*. This book—the first book devoted solely to expounding the doctrine of angels—was so important that some medieval theologians, such as Hugh of St. Victor (1096–1141), wrote commentaries on it. Because a convert of Paul was thought to be its author, the book was treated as the next best thing to the New Testament, and since it was far more detailed in its treatment of angels, it became *the* source of medieval angelology.

The Higher the Hierarchy, the Higher the Angel

According to Pseudo-Dionysius, the angelic spirits of heaven are organized into an elaborate hierarchical system. In a hierarchy, beings properly rule those below them and submit to those above them. A hierarchy is thus a kind of chain of command, as in the military. Medieval Europe saw hierarchy as the proper way of ordering a complex society. The Roman empire before its fall had been a hierarchy. The church had developed a hierarchical structure, with Christ at the top, then the bishop of Rome (who eventually became the pope), the bishops under the pope, the elders or presbyters (i.e., local congregational leaders) under the bishops, and the rest of the church membership under the presbyters.

That a well-ordered society would be hierarchical was not so much a doctrine for medieval Christians as it was an intuition or presupposition. Since heaven must be the ideally ordered society, it seemed obvious to medieval theologians that it must be organized in a perfect hierarchy.

In *Celestial Hierarchy*, the author asserts that there are nine orders of angelic beings, organized in groups of three into three

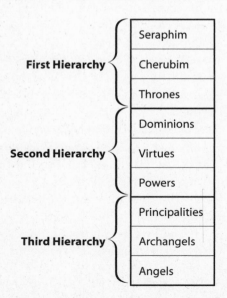

hierarchies. The higher up the order, the closer to God are the beings in that order. The beings on the top two rungs of the ladder are the seraphim and cherubim. (Those words are the plural forms of *seraph* and *cherub*; Hebrew masculine nouns are usually made plural by adding the suffix –*im*.) The beings on the bottom rung are the ones commonly called angels.

Pseudo-Dionysius seems to have been the first writer to come up with this nine-layer system of angelology. Roughly a century later, Gregory the Great (540–604) set forth a nearly identical system, and for the next eight hundred years or so European theologians rarely questioned it. Since some contemporary writers on angels still assume the basic validity of the nine-order classification,[1] we ought to compare it to the Bible.

Biblical Words for Heavenly Beings

The names of these nine orders of angels are taken directly from the Bible. The word "angels" is, of course, found frequently in the Bible. Five of the terms are taken from overlapping lists of spiritual powers in Paul's writings (Eph. 1:21; Col. 1:16); the word "virtue" derives from the Latin word *virtus*, used to translate the Greek word for "power" (*dynamis*) in Ephesians 1:21. Below is a table listing the biblical uses of these various words referring to spiritual powers.

One big problem for the medieval system is that no biblical passage refers to

> Although all of the words in angel-ranking appear in the Bible, the case against these words denoting nine distinct orders of heavenly beings is surprisingly strong.

the nine orders, either generally or with a list. Four of the words appear in Ephesians 1:21 and again in Colossians 1:16 (three of which appear in both verses). That's as close as it gets. According to Gregory the Great and many after him, in Jesus' parable of the lost coin (Luke 15:8–10) the nine coins that were not lost represent the nine orders of angels, and the tenth coin, which was lost, represents the human race.[2] If this is the best one can do, it's not much.

Name	References
Seraphim	Isaiah 6:2, 6
Cherubim	Gen. 3:24; Ex. 25:18 – 22; 26:1, 31; 36:35; 37:7 – 9; Num. 7:89; 1 Sam. 4:4; 2 Sam. 6:2; 22:11; 1 Kings 6:23 – 35; 7:29, 36; 8:6 – 7; 2 Kings 19:15; 1 Chron. 13:6; 28:18; 2 Chron. 3:7 – 14; 5:7 – 8; Pss. 18:10; 80:1; 99:1; Isa. 37:16; Ezek. 9:3; 10:1 – 9, 15 – 20; 11:22; 28:14, 16; 41:18 – 20, 25; Heb. 9:5
Thrones	Col. 1:16
Dominions	Eph. 1:21; Col. 1:16 (*kuriotētes*; cf. 2 Peter 2:10; Jude 8)
Virtues	Eph. 1:21 (*dynameis*; cf. Rom. 8:38; 1 Cor. 15:24; 1 Peter 3:22)
Powers	Eph. 1:21; 3:10; Col. 1:16 (*exousiai*; cf. 1 Cor. 15:24; Eph. 2:2; 6:12; Col. 1:13; 2:10, 15; 1 Peter 3:22)
Principalities	Eph. 1:21; 3:10; Col. 1:16 (*archai*; cf. Rom. 8:38; 1 Cor. 15:24; Eph. 6:12; Col. 2:10, 15; see also Jude 6)
Archangels	1 Thess. 4:16; Jude 9
Angels	Over 200 times in the Old Testament; about 40 times in the Apocrypha Over 60 times in the Gospels and Acts; 19 times in the Epistles; 50 times in Revelation

A second and rather serious difficulty for the theory that these nine terms refer to nine orders of heavenly angels is that at least some of these words, in Paul's epistles, refer in places to fallen or evil spirits. "For we do not wrestle against flesh and blood, but against principalities [*archas*], against powers [*exousias*], against the rulers of the darkness of this age, against spiritual hosts of wickedness in the heavenly places" (Eph. 6:12 NKJV; see also 1 Cor. 15:24;

Eph. 2:2; Col. 1:13; 2:15). Three of the five terms that come only from Paul's epistles sometimes have this reference to wicked spirits (see ch. 19).

Some of the problems with the medieval classification system arise from the descriptions the medieval theologians assigned to each order. For example, Pseudo-Dionysius classified the seraphim as the highest order of angelic beings and concluded that, as beings particularly devoted to the love of God, the seraphim never left God's presence. However, Isaiah 6:6–7 tells us that one of the seraphim flew to Isaiah. Rather than revise or abandon his hierarchical classification, Pseudo-Dionysius argued that the angel in question was not really a seraph but rather an angel acting on behalf of a seraph. Bonaventure and many other medieval theologians actually accepted this explanation. As Keck points out, "the quandary over this apparent glitch in the Dionysian system testifies both to the fragility of the system and the dedication of the angelologists who sought to keep the system together."[3]

Speaking of seraphim and cherubim, these are likely two different words for the same kind of angels. The word "seraphim" appears only in Isaiah's vision of God in Isaiah 6. They are described as having six wings, attending God on his throne, with some burning coals at hand, and crying, "Holy, Holy, Holy, is the LORD of hosts" (Isa. 6:3). In Ezekiel's visions of God, the prophet saw four cherubim, each having four wings, attending God on his throne, and with some burning coals at hand (Ezek. 1:1–6, 13, 22–28; 10:1–17). (In passing, we might note that these cherubim look nothing like the sweet, fat little babies depicted in Renaissance art!) John's vision of God on the throne combines elements from the visions of Isaiah

AUGUSTINE

Let those who are able answer these questions, if they can prove their answers to be true; but as for me, I confess my ignorance.... For what is the necessity for affirming, or denying, or defining with accuracy on these subjects, and other like them, when we may without blame be entirely ignorant of them?[4]

and Ezekiel; his "four living creatures" have six wings and cry, "Holy, holy, holy is the Lord God Almighty" (Rev. 4:2–8 NIV).

Given the difficulties with the nine-order angel classification system, it would have been better if medieval theologians had followed Augustine's example and admitted their "ignorance" of these matters. All we really know is that Jesus Christ is the Creator and Lord of the angels, that Michael is the captain of some or all of the good angels, and that angels perform different functions as God wills.

SENSE

There are different kinds of angels that do different things.

NONSENSE

We can classify angels by orders or ranks.

PART 3

WHAT ANGELS DO

Chapter 13

THE BODYGUARD

Angels can protect us from harm, but we don't have guardian angels assigned to us.

Popular interest in angels focuses above all else on the idea of guardian angels. Countless stories of angelic encounters reflect the belief that there are angels whose "job" is to protect us from harm.

Many religions have some idea of guardian spirits or angels, and the idea has had a long history in Christianity. One of the earliest Christian thinkers on record in support of belief in guardian angels was the third-century theologian Origen. A century later, Chrysostom, a renowned preacher, popularized the belief. In the thirteenth century, Thomas Aquinas developed a formal doctrine of guardian angels, and Catholics generally have accepted the idea ever since.

A few Christian theologians, notably Gregory of Nyssa in the fifth century, taught that each person has both a good angel assigned to him by God and a bad angel assigned to him by Satan. The idea survives to this day in popular culture, though more as a stock humorous image (the good angel and demon on either side of a person, whispering into his ears) than a sincerely held belief.

In the sixteenth century, John Calvin argued that Scripture did not clearly support the idea of personal guardian angels. Many Protestants, but by no means all, have followed him in regarding the idea with some suspicion.

So, are there guardian angels? In order to answer this question, we need to be sure we define our terms. The Bible clearly teaches that angels can protect people from harm and even intervene supernaturally to rescue people from danger. There's no question about *that*. The issue is whether God assigns each human being a particular angel whose ongoing job is to protect that person from harm. The *Encyclopedia of Angels* defines a guardian angel as "an angel who is attached to a person from birth to death, providing constant guidance, protection, and companionship."[1] This invisible bodyguard is what people generally mean by the term "guardian angel." In this chapter, we will consider the biblical passages that believers in guardian angels most often cite in support of the idea and see if it holds up.

Got Angel?

In Genesis 48:16, Jacob (now called Israel) spoke of "the angel who has redeemed me from all evil (NASB)." Not surprisingly, some people have thought Israel was referring to his guardian angel. However, as we saw in chapter 10, this "angel" was that mysterious figure known as "the angel of the LORD," or Jesus Christ appearing to human beings before he came to earth as a man. Let's look at this passage again:

> *The God* before whom my ancestors Abraham and Isaac walked,
> *The God* who has been my shepherd all my life to this day,
> *The angel* who has redeemed me from all evil,
> Bless the boys. (Gen. 48:15–16 NASB)

The first two lines call on Israel's God, and the third line is parallel to those lines. All three lines identify the One whom Israel asks to bless the two boys Ephraim and Manasseh. The verb for "bless" is a singular form, confirming that there is only One to whom Israel is appealing for the blessing. Therefore, this "angel" must be God, not a guardian angel.

Psalm 91:11 is a popular verse about angelic protection: "For He will give His angels charge concerning you, to guard you in all your ways." We will have more to say about this passage in the next chapter. Here, though, we simply need to point out why these are not guardian angels in the sense defined earlier. (1) These angels provide protection in response to God's charge or order. The psalmist is saying that God will order angels "to guard you," not that God has permanently assigned angels to guard people. (2) The psalmist is addressing an individual ("you" here is singular, not plural), yet this individual is promised protection by an unspecified but plural number of "angels." This statement, then, does not fit the model of one angel permanently assigned to guard one human being.

Catholics often appeal to the book of Tobit in support of the idea of a guardian angel. Tobit is one of a group of books that the Catholic Church accepts as part of the Old Testament but which Protestants do not accept. These books, known as the Apocrypha (meaning "hidden"), are not part of the Jewish Bible.[2] In Tobit, an archangel named Raphael accompanies a man named Tobit on a journey and reveals his true identity only at the end of the story. (The name Raphael does not appear anywhere in the undisputed books of the Old and New Testaments.) Even if there was no dispute about the place of the book of Tobit in the Bible, Raphael does not fit the mold of a guardian angel. He accompanies Tobit as a visible companion on a journey for a limited time, not as an invisible companion throughout his life.

The most popular proof texts for guardian angels come from the New Testament. In Matthew 18:10, Jesus, referring to children, spoke of "their angels in heaven." Many people think the fact that Jesus calls these beings "their angels" implies that God has assigned these angels to specific children. Here is what Jesus said:

> Truly I say to you, unless you are converted and become like children, you will not enter the kingdom of heaven. Whoever then humbles himself as this child, he is the greatest in the kingdom of heaven. And whoever receives one such child in My name receives Me; but whoever causes one of these little ones who believe in Me to stumble, it would be better for him to have a heavy millstone hung around his neck, and to be drowned in the depth of the sea....
>
> See that you do not despise one of these little ones, for I say to you that their angels in heaven continually see the face of My Father who is in heaven. (Matt. 18:3–6, 10 NASB)

Are these guardian angels? Well, if they are, they seem to be in the wrong place, because Jesus says they are "in heaven," not on earth shadowing their earthly charges. Moreover, instead of watching the children, Jesus says these angels "continually see the face of My Father who is in heaven."

Why, then, does Jesus call them "*their* angels"? Consider the context: Jesus is *not* assuring his disciples that angels will always protect little children from harm, but he is warning his disciples not to get children into trouble or look down on them. Given this context, the best explanation is that these angels are prepared to avenge those who despise or abuse the children. They are watching the Father's face in heaven, ready to respond immediately to any orders he may issue.

One passage in the Bible indicates that some people in the first century believed in guardian angels. In Acts 12, Luke tells us that the apostle Peter escaped from prison with the help of an angel and went to the house of Mark's mother, where a group of Christians was gathered to pray (12:6–12). (This passage was the inspiration for Amy Grant's popular Christian song "Angels Watching over Me.") When he knocked at the gate, a servant girl named Rhoda went to answer. As soon as she heard his voice, she became so excited that she ran inside to tell the others, leaving Peter waiting at the gate (vv. 13–14). Luke reports that they thought Rhoda was crazy and that, when she insisted, some said, "It is his angel" (v. 15).

Most commentators agree that this statement reflects a belief in guardian angels. Later Jewish writings suggest that at least some Jews believed that guardian angels looked like the people they protected. Moreover, as Ben Witherington notes, "it was believed that one's spirit or angel often lingered on earth, appearing for several days after one's death, and that belief may be reflected here."[3]

DUANE GARRETT

If "guardian angels" are meant, we have to wonder why these angels are in the Father's presence rather than down on earth, watching over their accident-prone little wards.[4]

However, Luke is *not* endorsing this idea of a guardian angel that looks like its charge. After all, he tells us that the person at the gate was really Peter, not his guardian angel. He reports that the people at the prayer meeting thought Rhoda was crazy, but that also was incorrect. As we mentioned in passing, Luke does tell us that an angel helped Peter escape from his jail cell. His description of the angel simply does not support the idea of a personal guardian angel. Luke says that "an angel of the Lord" led Peter out of the jail (Acts 12:7). After the angel had escorted him past all the guards and outside the prison gate to the street, "suddenly the angel left him" (v. 10). At this point Peter realized what had happened and said, "Now I am sure that the Lord has *sent forth his angel* and rescued me" (v. 11). The apostle Peter evidently did not think of this angel as his own guardian angel, but as an angel that God had specially dispatched to come rescue him.

Guardian Angels: Our "Invisible Friends"?

The idea of a personal bodyguard in the form of a guardian angel is not only popular; for many people it is a cherished belief, even one of great emotional comfort. In questioning the existence of guardian angels, we wish neither to offend nor to discourage. Nor is there any reason to be alarmed or to fear, since we are not in any way detracting from God's ability to protect his people. God does not need any angels to protect us, since he is omnipotent. God is pleased to give angels the responsibility and privilege of being his agents in protecting human beings as he wills. God can send large numbers of angels to protect any individual or group at any time that he chooses.

If we agree that God can and does send angels to protect people, why knock the idea of guardian angels? This is a fair question, and actually an important one. In addition to its not being an idea supported by Scripture, we have at least two other reasons for putting the guardian angel belief on the "nonsense" side of the ledger.

(1) Belief in guardian angels tends to foster the belief that we can and even should develop relationships with angels. Strictly speaking, there is no logical necessity why this should be so;

one could believe in guardian angels but also believe that they are usually unnoticed and will remain largely if not entirely unknown to us. In actual practice, though, most advocates of belief in guardian angels strongly encourage people to seek a close relationship with their angels. Here are just two examples:

Eileen Elias Freeman: "Angels want to be our friends. They are companions on the journey of life on this planet, ancient fellow travelers, whose love and light and wisdom can enrich our lives immeasurably."[5]

Terry Lynn Taylor: "Basically, I'm suggesting that you become best friends with your guardian angel! Pretend you have an invisible best friend who witnesses everything you experience and with whom you can share insights."[6]

Taylor's advice well represents the potential for self-deception here. She actually encourages people to pretend they have "an invisible best friend." When children make up invisible playmates on their own, it is generally cute, harmless, and even therapeutic. When adults recommend to other adults that they pretend to have an invisible friend who will protect them day and night as a guardian angel, that's bad advice. Taylor is simply saying explicitly what most guardian angel teaching implies, which is that a relationship with one's guardian angel begins in the imagination.

It gets worse. Since most people have never had any overt contact with an angel, how does one pursue an "intimate relationship" with one's guardian angel? Some angel experts offer specific instructions in how to make contact with one's angel. For example, Freeman encourages the use of visualization to invite angels to reveal themselves.[7] She even reports having used "guided meditation" to lead a married couple into visualizing their guardian angels to help them repair their marriage. To do this, they were told "to visualize the dark angels ... being soundly defeated by Michael and his angels of light."[8] The guided meditation ended with Freeman informing the couple that the light around them had changed color "from protective blue to radiant gold and white."[9] We hate to say it, but the visualization Freeman is recommending here is a form of occultism.

(2) A final reason for denying the existence of guardian angels is that the belief sets up a false expectation of constant protection. This error does follow logically from the very idea of guardian angels. If you have an angel personally assigned to shadow you in order to protect you and you get hurt or get into trouble of any kind, there is only one way you can explain this: it's your fault. Of course, it may be; but on the other hand, it may not be. But if the angel is there to protect you as long as you satisfy certain conditions, there is little choice but to conclude that you must be at fault.

Admittedly, some people do conclude that angelic protection is always available and therefore people who get hurt are simply not doing their part. Is this so? We will address this question in the next chapter.

SENSE
God can send angels to protect people whenever he chooses.

NONSENSE
We have guardian angels permanently assigned to protect us.

Chapter 14

SOMETIMES THE ANGELS JUST WATCH

God does not guarantee that angels will always protect us.

If angels are always on the job, should we conclude that anything bad that happens to us is our fault? We should—*if* there are angels whose job descriptions include guaranteeing our safety as long as we do our part. After all, we certainly agree that God's holy angels never fail to hold up their responsibilities.

At this point, many people wonder: Doesn't the Bible explicitly promise such unfailing angelic protection? There is one biblical passage that seems to make such a blanket promise—Psalm 91:11, a verse on which we commented briefly in the preceding chapter. In this chapter, we will take a closer look at Psalm 91 and note what other passages in the Bible say on this subject.

What's a Psalm For?

Let's put the reference to angels in Psalm 91:11 in a little context:

No evil will befall you,
Nor will any plague come near your tent.
For He will give His angels charge concerning you,
To guard you in all your ways.
They will bear you up in their hands,

That you do not strike your foot against a stone.
You will tread upon the lion and cobra,
The young lion and the serpent you will trample down.
(Ps. 91:10 – 13 NASB)

The psalmist's statement that "no evil will befall you" because God will charge his angels "to guard you in all your ways ... that you do not strike your foot against a stone" certainly sounds like "comprehensive collision coverage" — even better, since it sounds like a guarantee to *prevent* collision as minor as stubbing one's toe. It is not surprising that many people see this passage as proof that we always have angels protecting us.

The assumption that Christians often bring to this passage, as to the Old Testament in general, is that it is a promise directly from God to them. That is, when the psalmist says "you," Christians quite easily think, "That means *me*." Sometimes we can read the Psalms in this way and not get into trouble, but it is the wrong way to read the Psalms.

David and other men wrote the Psalms under the old covenant, God's binding relationship with Israel that he formed with them through Moses. They talked about what God did and would do for Israel (e.g., Pss. 68; 78; 105; 106; 135; and 136). Often they spoke more narrowly about what God did and would do for Jerusalem (e.g., Pss. 48; 79; 87; 122; and 147) or for Jerusalem's king, that is, David or his descendants (e.g., Pss. 2; 18; 22; 45; 72; 89; 110; and 132). The focus in these psalms is typically on the physical miracles God did

> When the psalmist says "you," Christians quite easily think, "That means me." Sometimes we can read a specific psalm in this way and not get into trouble, but in general it is the wrong way to read the Psalms.

for Israel and the physical blessings God gave to Jerusalem and to David. This focus was appropriate because the purpose of the old covenant was to create and sustain a physical nation from which the Messiah would come.

Under the inspiration of the Holy Spirit, what the psalmists wrote often foreshadowed or prophetically anticipated what God was going to do in and through David's greatest descendant, Jesus the Messiah (or Christ). Most Christians can see this easily in Psalm 22, where David's prayer for deliverance when he felt abandoned by God pictures Jesus' suffering on the cross (see Matt. 27:35–46, where Jesus quotes the first line of Ps. 22).[1] The physical blessings given to Israel and Israel's king pictured the spiritual blessings that God was going to give to people of all nations through Christ. The physical sufferings of which the Psalms speak often anticipate the suffering of Jesus for our sins, and the physical deliverance of which the Psalms speak often anticipate the resurrection of Jesus and the new life we have through faith in him.

The apostle Peter established this principle in the first Christian sermon, when he explained that in Psalm 16 David was not speaking ultimately about his own escape from death but about Jesus' resurrection from the dead (Acts 2:25–32; cf. Ps. 16:8–11). Although Christians experience suffering now, they look forward to an eternity of perfect physical and spiritual life awaiting them in their own resurrection (Rom. 8:18–23).

Angels Watching over — Me?

Now let's look at Psalm 91 again. In its Old Testament, Israelite context, the psalm is speaking about the physical protection that an Israelite will enjoy if he or she trusts completely in the Lord (Ps. 91:1–10). The description is idealized, even hyperbolic,[2] if one applies it to every Israelite. However, the psalmist never says that he is referring to all Israelites, and he even seems to distinguish himself ("I") from the one to whom this complete protection will apply (the singular "you"). He describes the protected one in language that David often used of himself (e.g., compare Ps. 91:1–4 with 18:1–3), which suggests that the psalmist is here speaking of David or his future descendant, the Messiah. In a physical sense, David was protected from all sorts of dangers, including literal lions (1 Sam. 17:34–37). In another psalm, David expresses confidence in God's deliverance from all dangers and the protection of the army of "the angel of the LORD" (Ps. 34:6–7).

In its original context in the Old Testament setting, then, Psalm 91 appears to speak most directly of David, and perhaps in a general or hyperbolic way of the protection God promised to the people of Israel if they would trust in him completely. That the psalmist also refers to or at least alludes to the Messiah is almost certain from verse 13, where he says, "You will tread upon the lion and cobra, the young lion and the serpent you will trample down" (NASB).

The image of treading or trampling on a cobra or serpent is a clear allusion to the first messianic promise in the Bible. After Adam and Eve succumbed to the temptation of Satan in the garden of Eden, God told Satan—who had taken the form of a serpent (Gen. 3:1, 14)—that the woman's "offspring" or descendant "will strike your head" (3:15). In Isaiah, prophetic visions of the future restoration of paradise through the Messiah picture a world without the serpent, or one in which the serpent is forced, as we might put it, to "eat dust" (Isa. 11:8; 65:25). Because of David's prowess in defeating lions that attacked his father's flock of sheep (1 Sam. 17:34–37), Isaiah also could picture the messianic paradise as one without any lions (Isa. 35:9) or where the lion had been completely tamed (11:6–7; 65:25).

We should read Psalm 91:13, then, as looking forward to the coming of Jesus the Messiah, through whom God is giving us victory over Satan and the rest of the forces of evil. In the New Testament, Jesus told his disciples that he had given them "authority to tread on serpents and scorpions, and over all the power of the enemy, and nothing will injure you" (Luke 10:19 NASB). He is not talking here about physical serpents or physical injury, but about authority over "the spirits" (v. 20), enabling his followers to cast out demons (v. 17).

Of course, Jesus suffered and died, as did many of his disciples later. Psalm 91 clearly cannot mean that God promised to protect the Messiah from all physical harm. What it can and does mean is that God's protection over the Messiah guaranteed that no one could inflict any harm on Jesus prior to his voluntarily submitting to his redemptive suffering and death. An angel protected Jesus from attempts to kill him early in his human life (Matt. 2:13, 19), and he survived several threats and attempts on his life during his public ministry (Luke 4:28–30; John 5:18; 8:59; 10:31, 39). Jesus asserted that when it came time for him to die, it would be by his choice; no one would be able to take his life away from him (John 10:17–18).

After submitting to that death for our sake, Jesus rose from the dead to unending, perfect life—the ultimate fulfillment of God's promise of "long life" (Ps. 91:16; cf. 16:11 and Acts 2:25–32). Likewise, we are not yet immune from physical suffering or death. Psalm 91 is not a promise of physical protection for us in this mortal life. Yet, through Jesus God frees us from Satan and the death grip of sin and promises us an eternal future of perfect, glorious life in the resurrection.

You may be wondering if the New Testament ever quotes Psalm 91:11. It does—but in an interesting and ironic twist, Satan quotes it as one of his three temptations of Jesus in the wilderness:

> Then the devil took him to the holy city and placed him on the pinnacle of the temple, and said to him, "If you are the Son of God, throw yourself down; for it is written,
>
> 'He will command his angels concerning you';
> and
>
> 'On their hands they will bear you up,
> So that you will not dash your foot against a stone.'"
>
> Jesus said to him, "Again, it is written, 'Do not put the Lord your God to the test.'" (Matt. 4:5–7; see also Luke 4:9–12)

Satan did not choose Psalm 91:11–12 at random. All three of his temptations related to Jesus' role as the messianic Son of God. The Devil tempted Jesus to provide miraculous bread for himself in the wilderness (reminiscent of the manna God had provided Israel in the wilderness through Moses), to summon the angels to protect him in dramatic "fulfillment" of Scripture, and to take power over all the kingdoms of the world. Jesus' response to all three temptations is to quote statements from Deuteronomy about the need to believe, trust, and worship the Lord God alone (Deut. 6:13, 16; 8:3).

That is what Israel was supposed (but in general failed) to do; it is what Jesus did perfectly on our behalf. As Jesus pointed out later, at any time he could have asked the Father to put at his disposal "more than twelve legions of angels" (Matt. 26:53), but when the time came, he freely chose to suffer and die for our sake (John 10:17–18). All the angels could do was watch. They stood by and awaited the time for the vindication of the Son of God when he rose from the grave and triumphed over Satan, sin, suffering, and death for us.

The message of Psalm 91:11 for Christians, then, is not that God has given us a carte blanche guarantee that angels will protect us from all harm. Sometimes bad things happen to us, and we're not to blame. The message of 91:11 is that God has acted through Jesus Christ to deliver us from the Devil and all spiritual harm, and he promises us that in the resurrection we will enjoy an eternal life free from all harm of any kind. In the meantime, God can and does send his angels to protect people when and as he chooses, but only as a foretaste or glimpse of the perfect life to which we look forward.

Angels Standing By

Elsewhere in the Bible, we find that God sometimes delivers people from harm through his angels and sometimes he does not. When Nebuchadnezzar ordered his soldiers to put Daniel's three friends into a furnace, the young men told the king, "If we are thrown into the blazing furnace, the God whom we serve is able to save us. He will rescue us from your power, Your Majesty" (Dan. 3:17 NLT). Then they added, "*But even if he doesn't*, Your Majesty can be sure that we will never serve your gods or worship the gold statue you have set up" (v. 18 NLT). They were confident in God and knew that one way or the other, God would deliver them from the king; but they also accepted the possibility that God would not spare them from death in the fiery furnace.

In this instance, God did protect these three friends of Daniel from the fire. However, as the writer of Hebrews points out, those

Old Testament believers who suffered torture, imprisonment, and even death out of loyalty to the Lord did so "by faith," just as much as those who escaped from lions, fire, and the sword (Heb. 11:32–40).

Incidentally, Nebuchadnezzar mentioned that he saw a fourth man in the furnace that looked like "the Son of God" (Dan. 3:25 NKJV; possibly "a son of the gods," NIV).[3] This figure may very well have been an angel (the ancient Greek translations of the passage actually read "like an angel of God"). It is also possible that this was another Old Testament appearance of the Son of God.

We commented in the previous chapter on Peter's miraculous deliverance from prison by the help of an angel (Acts 12:7–11). What we need to remember, though, is that James the brother of John had just been executed (12:2). As an apostle, James certainly would have been able to procure angelic deliverance for himself if that were something guaranteed believers. Yet James died. It is true that the church prayed for Peter (v. 5) whereas Luke says nothing about their praying for James. We may indeed see here an encouragement to prayer, but there is no reason to suppose that the church failed in James's case. It appears that Herod had James summarily executed, while leaving Peter to languish in prison for a time.

Moreover, the fact that the prayer group scoffed when Rhoda the maid told them that Peter was at the gate (Acts 12:15) suggests that Peter's deliverance cannot be credited to their faith. The bottom line is that sometimes God delivers his people from physical harm, and sometimes he does not.

Finally, in his first epistle to the church at Corinth, Paul scolded the believers there for thinking that they were so "spiritual" that they were living on top of the world, while Paul and others in apostolic ministry were suffering greatly for the cause of Christ. Paul told them, "We have become a spectacle to the entire world — to people and angels alike" (1 Cor. 4:9 NLT). In other words, Paul is saying that he and the other apostles often suffered while the angels just watched. If this can happen to God's faithful servants on the "front lines," we should not be discouraged in our faith if it happens to us.

SENSE

God sometimes sends his angels to deliver people
from harm.

NONSENSE

If angels do not rescue us from harm, it must be
our fault.

Chapter 15

ENTERTAINING ANGELS

Angelic appearances are rare, usually of cosmic importance, and not something to seek.

S o when was the last time you saw or talked to an angel?

In the opinion of some people, we should all encounter angels at least occasionally if not frequently. According to Doreen Virtue, *"those who are willing and ready to see angels will see angels."*[1] Karen Goldman asserts, "Angels are speaking to everyone. Some of us are only listening better."[2] Proponents like these regale us with story after story of encounters with angels. It's enough to make a person wonder: Why don't I run into an angel once in a while?

The question here is not whether angels are invisibly present around us, acting behind the scenes. The Bible is clear that this is so. Nor are we questioning the possibility of angels appearing to people today. Of course they might. What we are questioning is the claim that overt encounters with angels — either seeing them or communicating with them — is something that should happen to everyone and can happen to anyone with great frequency. This claim simply is not biblical, as we will show.

When Angels Came Calling

Let's start by reviewing the biblical accounts in which human beings actually saw an angel (including appearances of "the angel of the

People in the Bible Who Saw Angels or "the Angel of the LORD"		
Hagar (2 times) (Gen. 16:7–13; 21:16–18)	Elijah (2 times) (1 Kings 19:5–7; 2 Kings 1:3)	Joseph (3 times, in dreams) (Matt. 1:20; 2:13, 19)
Abraham (2 times) (Gen. 18; 22:9–18)	Elisha (2 Kings 6:15–17)	Shepherds (at Jesus' birth) (Luke 2:8–14)
Lot and his family (Gen. 19)	David (1 Chron. 21:16–18)	Jesus (2 times) (Mark 1:13; Luke 22:43)
Jacob (3 times) (Gen. 28:1; 32:1, 24–30)	Isaiah (Isa. 6:2)	The women at the tomb (Matt. 28:2–5 and parallels)
Moses (Ex. 3:2–6)	Ezekiel (in several visions) (especially Ezek. 1; 10)	The apostles (2 times) (Acts 1:10–11; 5:19)
Balaam (and his donkey!) (Num. 22:22–35)	Daniel (Dan. 6:22)	Philip (Acts 8:26)
Joshua (Josh. 5:13–15)	Daniel's three friends (Dan. 3:25)	Cornelius (Acts 10:3–7)
The people of Israel (Judg. 2:1–4)	Nebuchadnezzar (Dan. 3:25; 4:13, 17, 23)	Peter (Acts 12:7–11)
Gideon (Judg. 6:11–18)	Zacharias (or Zechariah) (Luke 1:11–20)	Paul (Acts 27:23–24)
Samson's parents (Judg. 13:3–23)	Mary (Luke 1:26–38)	John (several visions) (throughout Revelation)

LORD"). The list is rather short (see the table above). Of course, it is possible and even likely that angels appeared to people on other occasions not mentioned in the Bible. Still, we may fairly consider the biblical record *representative* of angelic appearances to God's people.

(1) The first thing to notice is that most of the biblical figures who saw angels apparently saw them only once. The Gospels only

report Jesus having overt interaction with angels on two occasions. Three separate encounters with angels are the most reported for any individual (except for John, who had a series of encounters with angels in the book of Revelation), and these usually involved dreams or visions.

(2) Every appearance of an angel had something to do with the formation and survival of the covenant people of God and the bringing of salvation to the world. The Bible simply does not tell stories of angels appearing at random to help people in times of need or to communicate comforting messages to the suffering. Angels appeared or communicated with human beings for a variety of reasons, all of which related to the unfolding history of redemption:

- Announcing the miraculous birth of a key figure (Abraham, Samson's parents, Zacharias, Mary and Joseph, the shepherds)
- Protecting family members of the patriarchs (Hagar and Ishmael, Lot, Isaac [Gen. 22:9–18])
- Calling prophets and other leaders to ministry (Moses, Gideon, Isaiah, Ezekiel)
- Giving assurance of God's fulfillment of his covenant promises (Jacob, Joshua)
- Delivering or strengthening prophets and other key figures (Elijah, Elisha, Daniel and his friends, Jesus, the apostles, Peter, Paul)
- Warning of chastisement or judgment from God relating to Israel or its enemies (Balaam, people of Israel, David, Nebuchadnezzar)
- Announcing Jesus' resurrection (the women at the tomb)
- Directing the expansion of the church to new groups of people (Philip, Cornelius)
- Revealing God's purposes for his people in the future (Ezekiel, John)

Again, it is reasonable to suppose that angels appeared on other occasions that the Bible does not happen to record. Even so, the evidence from the Bible makes it clear that angelic encounters were rare and usually of great significance in the larger scheme of things.

(3) Another important point is that almost all of these angelic appearances were a surprise. Most of the biblical accounts explicitly mention the fact that the people who saw angels were surprised and even fearful of them. There is a subtle but important difference in this regard between biblical angel encounters and many modern angel stories. In a typical modern angel story, angels come to people who are fearful because of their circumstances (e.g., they may be afraid of dying, or afraid of being alone) and offer them comfort. In the typical biblical angel story, angels come to people who are going about their business and the angels have to tell them not to be afraid *of them*.

(4) Furthermore, most of the people in the Bible who saw angels were not notable in their spiritual sensitivity (Jesus being the obvious exception, and perhaps a few others to a lesser degree). In no such instance does anyone seek an encounter with angels. No human being prays to an angel, asks God to send an angel, or engages in any sort of spiritual or religious regimen or activity in order to open the door to encounters with angels. No biblical text ever suggests that believers ought to call on angels, speak to angels, or seek or even expect angelic encounters.

Some teachers have gone to extreme lengths to find precedent in the Bible for seeking angelic contact or support. As we noted in the preceding chapter, when men sent by the Jewish leadership arrested Jesus, he reminded his disciples that he could at any time ask the Father "and He will at once put at My disposal more than twelve legions of angels" (Matt. 26:53 NASB). One televangelist has appealed to this statement to prove that every believer has at least 40,000 guardian angels.[3] (Twelve legions would number about 72,000 soldiers, but who's counting?) Supposedly, if Jesus could

C. S. LEWIS

In Scripture the visitation of an angel is always alarming; it has to begin by saying, "Fear not." The Victorian angel looks as if it were going to say, "There, there."[4]

have thousands of angels at his disposal, we can too. But Jesus' unique identity as the Son of God and ruler of the angels (see Heb. 1:6) ought to be enough to dispense with this interpretation.

Additionally, we would point out that Jesus did not claim that the angels were *already* at his disposal but that the Father could make them so if Jesus asked. What we have here, then, is an instance of the unique Son of God in a crucially important turning point in his life and in human history saying that he *could* ask the Father to make angels available to him but that he will *not*. It is hardly plausible to view this incident as evidence that Christians have angels waiting to intervene if only they have enough faith.

Entertaining Angels Unawares?

Toward the end of the book of Hebrews, the writer says, "Do not neglect to show hospitality to strangers, for by doing that some have entertained angels without knowing it" (Heb. 13:2; the KJV says, "some have entertained angels unawares"). Some Christians understand this verse to imply that ordinary-looking persons whom they meet may frequently turn out to be angels. They see Hebrews 13:2 as encouraging the belief that encounters with angels may be common. One writer suggests that this text "tells us we have probably ALL seen angels at some time in our lives—without knowing it."[5]

Before assessing this implication, we should try to understand what the writer of Hebrews[6] means when he says that "some have entertained angels without knowing it." Most biblical scholars agree that Hebrews 13:2 is alluding to the accounts in Genesis 18–19 of Abraham and his nephew Lot showing hospitality to angels. Failure to show "hospitality to strangers" was a major reason why God condemned Sodom and Gomorrah to destruction. The writer of Hebrews had just referred to God as "a consuming fire" (12:29), recalling the destruction of the cities with fire and brimstone; and he goes on in the immediate context to urge that marriage be honored, "for God will judge fornicators and adulterers" (13:4), recalling the gross sexual sins with which Sodom was also associated.

A close reading of Genesis 18–19 supports this interpretation of Hebrews 13:2. After the Lord and the two angels meet with Abraham, the two angels leave for Sodom while the Lord reveals to Abraham the judgment about to come on Sodom (Gen. 18). Lot meets the two angels and invites them to spend the night at his house before going on their way (19:1–2). Clearly, at this point he does not know they are angels. Only after the two strangers strike the townsmen with blindness and tell Lot that they are about to bring God's judgment on the city (19:11–13) would Lot have known that they were angels from God.

So what does Hebrews 13:2 tell us about visits from angels? Not much. The point of this verse is to encourage Christians to be hospitable, not to encourage them to be on the alert for angelic encounters. Nor does the text mean that strangers whom we meet and never see again might be angels. When the writer says that some "entertained angels without knowing it," he does not mean that the angels never made clear their true nature. When Abraham and Lot met the strangers, they did not know they were angels, but they certainly knew they were before the visitors disappeared. Moreover, once we understand that this verse is alluding to angelic visits involving judgment, we will not read it as encouraging us to look for angels in our daily lives.

Are we saying angels never appear to people today? No. The Bible never says angelic visitations had stopped, nor is there any reason why they should stop entirely. But angels appeared or spoke to people in the Bible only on rare occasions. It is reasonable to infer from the biblical data that angelic visitations today will be extremely rare. If you never see an angel in this lifetime, don't take that as a sign of anything being wrong with you spiritually.

SENSE

Angels appeared to people in the Bible and they might do so today.

NONSENSE

We should all expect to encounter angels.

Chapter 16

PUTTING ANGEL STORIES TO THE TEST

Here's what to look for in a story about an encounter with a real angel.

It is safe to say that people rarely encounter angels today. We can make that statement safely because, as we saw in the previous chapter, angelic encounters have *always* been rare, even during biblical times. Yet we cannot say that angels *never* appear to or interact with people today. They still exist, they still are active (though nearly always invisibly), and there's nothing to prevent angels from appearing to people whenever God wants.

We want to balance two legitimate concerns. On the one hand, we want to affirm the honest experiences of people who sincerely report encountering angels and to acknowledge the positive impact such experiences can have. On the other hand, we want to reject erroneous reports about angels and to make sure that such reports do not deceive people into straying from the truth.

In short, what we need is *discernment*—an ability to tell the true from the false, the good from the bad, in stories about angels.

The Good, the Bad, and the "Uh ..."

Whenever someone (you or anyone else) thinks he[1] has encountered an angel, realize that you do not have to choose between agreeing that he saw an angel and calling him a liar.[2] There are actually five possibilities:[3]

1. He saw a human being (and mistook that human for an angel).
2. He was mistaken—he did not see anyone.
3. He lied—he did not see anyone.
4. He saw an actual, good angel.
5. He saw an actual angel, but it was a demon (fallen angel).

Angel Sightings: Charting the Possibilities

He reports seeing an angel

He really saw someone / He did not see anyone

(1) He saw a human being / He saw a supernatural being

(2) He was mistaken / 3) He lied

(4) He saw a good angel / (5) He saw a bad angel (demon)

Our study of what the Bible says about angel appearances leads us to expect that most (but not all) such reports today will fall into one of the first three options. We number these three options in the order we think most common; in other words, we think in most cases the reporters (1) actually saw a human being rather than an angel, and that it is more likely that those reporting angel sightings who did not see a human being (2) are mistaken than that (3) they are lying. The last two options—seeing a good angel or seeing a demon—are both likely to be so rare that it would be difficult to guess which one is more common.

We should also caution that it is not always possible to reach a definite, certain conclusion about each reported angel sighting. Sometimes we can be reasonably sure about our answer, but in many cases we just do not have enough information. It is wisest in such instances to admit that we don't know.

Don't Fall for These "Proofs"

Those who endorse angel stories often claim they have certain marks or characteristics that prove they are genuine encounters with angels. Let's consider some of these characteristics and determine whether they inevitably demonstrate a genuine encounter.

(1) *The angel is a figure of bright light.* Naturally, if a demon wanted to pose as an angel, he'd put on his "Sunday best." Just as wicked men usually cultivate an image of respectability and even high ideals, wicked spirits try to pass themselves off as angels of light (see 2 Cor. 11:14).

(2) *The angel seems to be good.* Same song, second verse as the "proof" we just considered (see 2 Cor. 11:15). Bad angels don't wear black hats, much less red suits with horns; they don't brandish pitchforks; and they usually claim to want to help us.

(3) *The angel claims to be from God or from heaven.* Same song, third verse (see Gal. 1:8); rare is the demon whose stated mailing address is "Hell."

(4) *The angel quotes the Bible.* Unfortunately, the Devil can quote Scripture, though he takes it out of context (Matt. 4:6; Luke 4:9–11).

(5) *The angel does something amazing.* Even false prophets occasionally make an accurate prediction; that's no reason to trust them (Deut. 13:1–5). Likewise, when a miracle apparently occurs, we should not automatically assume that God or an angel did it (see Matt. 24:24; 2 Thess. 2:9).

(6) *The "angel" mysteriously disappears.* In many contemporary angel stories, one feature seems to recur more than any other. After offering some comforting words or tangible assistance, a stranger seems to disappear. We're not talking about a person vanishing while someone is intently looking at them. Rather, in these stories the helpful stranger "disappears" while no one is looking. Those who report these incidents usually assert that the stranger (or, in some stories, his car or truck) got away too quickly to have done so naturally, or that had he left in a natural manner they would have noticed.

The vast majority of these stories are likely to be sincere reports of helpful actions by strangers who were human beings, not angels.

In a crisis, people around us can seem to come or go suddenly because we have a distorted perception of our surroundings. The strangers sometimes "disappear" because they are "Good Samaritans" who slip away quietly simply because they don't want to draw attention to themselves. We realize that some of these occurrences may involve actual angels, but we would advise against treating the "quick getaway" as a proof.

Proving It Was *Not* an Angel

It is actually easier to prove that a reported angel encounter did *not* involve one of God's angels than to prove that it *was* an angel. The Bible gives us a number of important negative tests that we can apply to angel stories. A *negative test* can prove that something is not true; these tests can prove that a good angel did not appear.

(1) *Angels whose messages conflict with Scripture are either demonic or imagined* (Gal. 1:8; 2 Cor. 11:14; 1 Tim. 4:1; 1 John 4:1). This is the easiest test to apply and exposes some of the most famous angel stories in history as untrustworthy. For example, Muhammad reported that the angel Gabriel appeared to him and told him to recite some revelations from God that became the Qur'an, the holy book of Islam. The Qur'an, however, denies that Jesus is the Son of God and that he died for our sins.

Similarly, Joseph Smith reported that an angel by the name of Moroni gave him the golden plates that supposedly contained the Book of Mormon, leading him eventually to found the Mormon Church. The Book of Mormon teaches that the Bible is corrupt and an insufficient basis for Christian doctrine.

We may confidently conclude that Muhammad and Joseph did not see a legitimate angel from heaven. Note, though, that it is not as easy to determine what Muhammad and Joseph did see. Did they make it up? Did they see a demon? Were they deluded? It's hard to say.

(2) *Angels that introduce new doctrines or new practices into Christianity are not from God.* Even if a new doctrine does not seem directly contrary to Scripture, the time for new teaching is past.

God has told us in the New Testament what we need to believe and how we need to live. We already have "the faith which was once for all handed down to the saints" (Jude 3 NASB); the church's foundation of truth is the body of revelation that Jesus Christ gave us through his apostles and prophets (Eph. 2:20; 3:5).

(3) *Angels who encourage or permit worship or excessive devotion to angels are not from God* (Col. 2:18; Rev. 19:10; 22:8–9). Most angel devotees, of course, deny worshiping angels. However, if they talk to angels daily, speak about angels in reverential or adulatory ways, make shrines to angels, or in other ways give angels extreme or undue attention, such behavior proves their encounters with angels are imagined or demonic.

(4) *Angels who claim to be departed human beings are not from God.* This follows, obviously, from the fact that angels are not departed human beings (see ch. 8).

(5) *Angels who leave unbelievers with a feeling of peace or spiritual security are not from God.* According to the Bible, those who do not yet believe in Jesus Christ need to do so in order to have peace with God—in order to be reconciled to God (Rom. 5:1–11). Thus, even if an angel says nothing overtly wrong, if his appearance evokes in non-Christians a sense of spiritual tranquility, then the angel is not from God.

In addition to these directly biblical tests, we can often discern that reports of angels are unreliable, based on what we know about angels from the Bible:

(1) *Persons who report seeing angels on numerous occasions are probably mistaken or deceiving others.* As we have seen, even Jesus and other leading figures in the Bible saw angels only a few times in their lives. Some angel book authors claim to have seen angels dozens and even hundreds of times.

(2) *Persons whose descriptions of angels go far beyond biblical parameters are probably mistaken or deceiving others.* No one in the Bible ever describes an angel in any significant detail. Yet many angel stories today include details about an alleged angel's hair and eye color, height, style and color of clothing, and especially gender. We suggest suspicion is in order with regard to any story of an angel

as overtly female in form or appearance. Similarly, we should be skeptical of any description of angels as highly sensuous, whether male or female.

(3) *Persons who report long conversations with angels are probably deceived or deceiving others.* In the Bible, angelic appearances are brief, as are their messages. People who report hours of conversation with angels or who claim that angels have dictated pages and pages of material to them should not be trusted. It is probably unrealistic to think that the person reporting these encounters saw a human being and mistook him for an angel. Most likely, either the person reporting these angelic communications is lying or has encountered a demonic spirit.

Positive Identification

When do we have good reason to conclude that someone has encountered a real angel from God? Angel stories should pass the following tests.

(1) *No "red flags."* A good angel story will pass all of the above negative tests. It will not contradict or add to Scripture or represent angels in a way at odds with the Bible. We may conclude that encounters that pass this test were not demonic deceptions or human fabrications.

(2) *Naturally inexplicable.* In the Bible, angelic visitations were always unmistakable, at least by the time they ended. Typically, the angel identified himself as an angel and said or did something that is naturally impossible. This test is crucial for determining whether the encounter in question was of a supernatural being.

It is not necessary or realistic to demand a "scientific" verification of the natural impossibility of the event. Angels don't stand around waiting for researchers in lab coats to run controlled experiments. Still, the discerning person will want to have *some* reason to view the incident as supernatural. An experience in which a person sees no one but "feels" something, or in which a person narrowly or amazingly avoids injury or death, may or may not be the work of an angel. Unless there is some overt evidence for the supernatural, it is best to suspend judgment.

(3) *Glorifying to Jesus Christ.* This test is implicit in the negative tests but is too important not to make explicit. Angel stories should not merely give lip service to Jesus; they should exalt Jesus as "Christ the Lord" (Luke 2:11). Angels expect the Lord to get the credit (see Acts 12:11, 17).

(4) *Verifiable.* Many if not most angel stories are beyond verification. There is probably no way for us to know if Johnnie really saw an angel in his bedroom when he was four years old and his beloved grandmother had passed away. (We're positive it wasn't Grandma, though.) For Johnnie, though, the experience is "verified" by virtue of its being his own. At the same time, some elements of angel stories are in principle verifiable. If a surgeon reports seeing an angel in an operating room during a difficult surgery, and the hospital confirms that the surgeon performed the operation and that the patient survived in a remarkable fashion, such information gives the report a great deal of credibility.

In sum: a healthy skepticism is in order when listening to angel stories. If an angel story can pass all four of the tests we have just explained, it is reasonable to believe that the story is true. Most angel stories cannot pass all four tests. A story that passes the first three tests (biblical, naturally inexplicable, and glorifying to Jesus Christ) is highly plausible but not proven. There is no harm in believing such accounts. If an angel story doesn't pass the first test, we should reject it outright.

SENSE

Some angel stories are credible; many are not.

NONSENSE

We should accept stories about angels as long as they are nice and talk about God and heaven.

PART 4

THE DEVIL AND HIS ANGELS

Chapter 17

YES, VIRGINIA, THERE REALLY IS A SATAN

The Devil does exist, though he doesn't mind if you disagree.

O ur focus in this book up to here has been on the good or holy angels — those spiritual beings who serve God loyally. But we have already mentioned repeatedly the existence of bad, wicked angels. If we are to have a sound, discerning view of the angels, we must inform ourselves about those evil angels and their leader, the Devil.

Does the Devil really exist? Not surprisingly, people skeptical of the existence of angels tend to doubt the existence of bad angels. We have already addressed some of the objections skeptics raise to the existence of angels (see ch. 2). There are two additional objections, however, to belief in the existence of the Devil and his minions that are worth considering.

The Devil of the Gaps?

One objection often raised is a sort of "Devil-of-the-gaps" objection. This is similar to the argument known as the "God-of-the-gaps" objection, according to which God is just a religious way of

CHARLES BAUDELAIRE

The Devil's deepest wile is to persuade us that he does not exist.

saying that we don't understand something. The general idea here is that it is a mistake to attribute a supernatural cause to a natural phenomenon. People made this mistake when they explained lightning as fire from the gods, or when they blamed all manner of mental illness on demons. The excuse, "The Devil made me do it," which TV comedian Flip Wilson turned into a stock joke in the 1970s, is one way of representing the mistake.

Our answer to the "Devil-of-the-gaps" objection is similar to our answer to the "God-of-the-gaps" argument. That answer is threefold.

(1) The fact that people have tended to attribute too much to direct supernatural intervention does not disprove the supernatural; it just proves that the supernatural is less "intrusive" than people thought.

(2) After a couple of centuries when the role of the supernatural seemed to be diminishing, the pendulum has begun swinging the other way. Scientists have started finding positive evidence for God as a supernatural, intelligent Creator. This evidence consists not of gaps in our knowledge, but of new information for which a supernatural Creator is *the best explanation*.[1] Likewise, some surprisingly rigorous investigations have yielded positive evidence for the existence of hostile supernatural forces. For example, careful research has shown that demonic possession is a real, if rare, phenomenon, and that it cannot be explained away as a natural psychiatric disorder. We will discuss some of this evidence in chapter 20.

(3) The most pervasive evidence for the supernatural is not evidence of direct intervention but of a transcendent or spiritual

C. S. LEWIS

There are two equal and opposite errors into which our race can fall about the devils. One is to disbelieve in their existence. The other is to believe, and to feel an excessive and unhealthy interest in them. They themselves are equally pleased by both errors, and hail a materialist or a magician with the same delight.[2]

dimension to existence. Thus, the most pervasive evidence for God's existence is not the occurrence of miracles (though they can count as evidence, too) but the fact that there is purpose and meaning in the world—and especially in human life. The world is not a cosmic accident, and human beings are here for a purpose and need to find and fulfill that purpose.

By contrast, the most pervasive evidence for the Devil's existence is not demonic possession (though that can count as evidence, too) but the otherwise incomprehensible perversity that human beings all too often exhibit. "Man's inhumanity to man" remains no less a mystery after centuries of scientific advances. Humanity is a species that is capable of moral reflection, of great altruism and heroism—and yet is also capable of deliberate, calculating evil.[3] Most of the time, the evil we do is explicable in terms of human emotions and motivations. Yet there is a nagging sense that forces beyond what we can see are manipulating us, and sometimes human evil is simply too horrible to understand. Without in any way shifting the blame away from ourselves, we ought to consider the possibility that the Bible is right and that evil supernatural beings have some part in the plot.

The Evolution of the Devil?

We have just mentioned the Bible's teaching about the Devil. The second objection to belief in the Devil attacks the reliability of that teaching. According to the conventional wisdom in certain circles of biblical scholarship, the Devil is a fictional character, developed late in biblical history. Old Testament references to Satan, they tell us, are sparse and do not portray him as the archenemy of God but as his loyal servant.[4]

MICHAEL GREEN

Doubt about the existence of a malign focus of evil is to be found, by and large, only in Christian lands.... It would be broadly true to say that disbelief in the devil is a characteristic only of materialistic Western Christendom.[5]

It is true that the Old Testament says little about Satan or about demons generally. There is a good reason for this. The culture in which the Israelites lived was polytheistic. The surrounding peoples believed in a variety of friendly and malevolent spirits, all of whom needed to be given their due in religious rituals if one wished to avoid trouble. The Old Testament writers go out of their way to put the existence of such spirits in their place. The only spirit to whom the Israelites were to accord any religious honors was the Lord God. Any other spirits were of less power and were under his control. Dennis Kinlaw explains:

> The Old Testament acknowledges the spirit world but seems bent upon minimizing, demythologizing, or marginalizing it. Wherever it does occur, it always has its origin in Yahweh and its role and domain determined by His sovereignty. No autonomous domain, independent of Yahweh, or outside His immediate control, exists to threaten man.... No concessions were to be made to the popular pressure to turn to the crutches of magic, idolatry, or the occult to deal with daily fears or anxieties.[6]

The Old Testament, then, downplays the power of evil spirits while acknowledging their existence. The same is true for the leader of the evil spirits.

The most detailed passage about Satan in the Old Testament is Job 1–2, which functions as the prologue to the book. After introducing Job as a righteous man, the book introduces Satan as a spirit who had been "roaming through the earth and going back and forth in it" (1:7; 2:2 NIV). He then appears in the heavenly council along with the "sons of God" (1:6 NIV, NASB), a term used in the Old Testament for angels. (The NRSV translates the expression as "the heavenly beings.") Scholars debate whether the book of Job portrays Satan as a "court-appointed" prosecutor or as intent on doing mischief. According to Elaine Pagels, Satan is "a member of the heavenly court, God's obedient servant."[7] However, this increasingly popular view of the Satan of Job is incorrect.

(1) Satan is clearly distinguished from the sons of God: "The sons of God came to present themselves before the LORD, and Satan also came among them" (Job 1:6 NASB).

(2) Satan and the Lord do not think highly of each other. Satan alleges that Job fears God only because God has given him so much (Job 1:9–11). As Sydney Page observes, "Satan implies that God is wrong in thinking so highly of Job and that he was wrong to reward Job's piety with prosperity."[8] For his part, the Lord tells Satan later that he had "incited" God against Job without cause (2:3).

(3) Satan's intentions toward Job appear evil. Page points out that God sets limits on the damage Satan can do to Job, implying that Satan would like to do malicious harm to Job.[9]

In short, Satan is disrespectful toward God and hostile toward human beings. The theory that Satan is just doing his job doesn't fit the text. Perhaps we should think of Satan as a kind of supernatural "ambulance chaser" or opportunistic "trial lawyer"—a being looking for people to accuse of wrongdoing. This picture is consistent with what we find in the rest of the Bible.

Some people take seriously the theory that the Devil is just doing his job as a belief that we should embrace today. (At least, we think they are serious!) The authors of *Ask Your Angels* actually claim that Satan volunteered for the job: "God asked for a volunteer among His top angels who might be willing to go down to Earth and help strengthen humanity's spiritual resolve by offering constant temptation. Lucifer volunteered."[10] According to Andrew Ramer, one of the three authors of *Ask Your Angels*, Lucifer told him:

> But the devil is only a mirror bearer, a representative of the family of angels whose function is to reveal to you not your beauty, but your capacity for evil.... Hitler, Stalin, the other monsters of your century—they were not tools of the devil, but men who feared to own about themselves what devils were trying to show them.[11]

What would you expect the Devil to say about himself?

Such "revelations" concerning the Devil are unreliable, to put it mildly. They are opinions offered without evidence. Taking Satan's word for his true purpose and intentions (assuming for the sake of argument that he really would grant Ramer an interview) seems the height of folly. The Bible's teaching on Satan, however, may be trusted because of the evidence that God inspired the Bible.[12] There is no more reliable — or sober — guide to thinking about the Devil.

SENSE
The Devil is real and is really bad.

NONSENSE
The Devil is a myth or a force for our self-improvement.

Chapter 18

THE DETAILS ON THE DEVIL

His names, what he's like, and what he can and cannot do.

W hat does the Bible teach about the Devil? As we will see, the Bible provides information about the Devil on a "need to know basis."

A Rogue by Any Other Name

The leader of the rebel angels goes by several names; the two best known, "Satan" and "the Devil," essentially mean the same thing.

The word *satan* actually means "adversary" in Hebrew. The Old Testament uses it to describe different enemies, human or not. In three passages, the Old Testament refers to a particular supernatural being as "the Satan" (Job 1–2; Zech. 3:1–2) or just "Satan" (1 Chron. 21:1). He is, in other words, *the* Adversary; he is Cosmic Enemy Number One.

The word *devil* comes from the Greek word *diabolos*, from which we also get our word "diabolical" (which means, in effect, anything worthy of the Devil). It is the word the Jews used to translate the Hebrew word *satan* in their Greek translations of the Old Testament. The New Testament uses both words to refer to the same arch-villain angel. We tend to use "Satan" as if it were his proper name and "the Devil" as if it were his official title. However, the two words mean essentially the same thing. The Bible never gives us what we would call a proper name for the Devil. In English, fallen angels in general are sometimes called "devils," but "the Devil" (capitalized or not) is their *Führer*.

The Unholy Spirit

Like the angels, the Devil is a spirit—an ethereal, immaterial being. He is "the ruler of the power of the air" (Eph. 2:2). He is therefore able to "disguise himself as an angel of light" (2 Cor. 11:14). Satan is a person, if you can call such an evil being that. The Bible describes him conversing with God in heaven (Job 1:6–12; 2:1–6) and with Jesus in the wilderness (Matt. 4:1–11).

A frequent title for Satan in the New Testament is "the evil one" (Matt. 5:37; 6:13; 13:19, 38; John 17:15; Eph. 6:16; 2 Thess. 3:3; 1 John 2:13–14; 3:12; 5:18–19). The Devil is clearly the epitome and architect of evil. He is also called "the tempter" (Matt. 4:3; 1 Thess. 3:5) and "the father of lies" (John 8:44). These descriptions, along with the title Satan/Devil, yield a consistent view of his modus operandi: his main activity is to lie to people in order to tempt them to do evil.

The Devil is also the leader of a horde of evil spirits, which are "his angels" (Matt. 25:41; Rev. 12:9). The Gospels and Acts describe these beings as "unclean spirits" some twenty times and as "demons" about fifty times. Luke also refers to them as "evil spirits" (Luke 7:21; 8:2; Acts 19:11–16). Jesus accepted the conventional Jewish belief of his day that the Devil—whom the Pharisees called Beelzebub—was the ruler of the demons (Matt. 12:24, 26–27; Mark 3:22–23, 26; Luke 11:15, 18–19). The name Beelzebub—or more properly, Beelzebul—derives in part from the name of a popular Canaanite deity in the Old Testament, Baal (see 2 Kings 1:2–6, 16).[1]

ALEX KONYA

Underestimating the Enemy is a tactical error in battle that inevitably leads to a crushing defeat.[2]

From what the Bible tells us about Satan, we can draw certain conclusions about his abilities. It is obvious that the Devil is a powerful and intelligent being. Jesus called the Devil "the ruler of this world" (John 12:31; 14:30; 16:11). The apostle Paul once referred to him as "the god of this age" who has blinded unbelievers (2 Cor. 4:4 NIV),[3] and the apostle John stated that "the whole world lies under the power of the evil one" (1 John 5:19). Paul also warned that Satan was capable of producing apparent miracles (2 Thess. 2:9).

Whatever these statements mean, they testify to Satan's power. We should also not underestimate his intelligence. Satan excels at twisting the truth in a seemingly reasonable manner. Recall, for example, Satan's clever misuse of Psalm 91 when tempting Jesus to prove he was God's Son (see ch. 14). Satan is the consummate schemer (2 Cor. 2:11; Eph. 6:11) and master of disguise (2 Cor. 11:14).

Nevertheless, it is important to remember that Satan is not in any sense God's equal—not even close. Whatever power the Devil has, he has received from God. When Satan wanted to hurt Job to destroy his faith, God limited what Satan could do to Job (Job 1:12; 2:6). Satan is also limited in what he can know; unlike God, the Devil does not know our hearts (cf. 1 Kings 8:39). Of course, like anyone else, Satan can often get a good idea of what we are thinking or feeling by simply observing us. Then again, Satan is not omnipresent; only God is everywhere at once and therefore only God can observe what is happening everywhere at the same time. Satan must therefore rely on his angels to see and do things in most places.

It follows that Satan is not really a god. He is a created being, limited in his knowledge, intelligence, power, and presence. Neither Satan nor his demons are gods in terms of their nature (1 Cor. 10:20–21; see also Gal. 4:8). Of course, it is always wrong to worship the Devil or any of the demons (Matt. 4:9–10; Rev. 9:20). They deserve no honor or respect from us.

Therefore, when Paul calls Satan "the god of this age" (2 Cor. 4:4 NIV), he is not suggesting that there is anything *legitimate* about Satan's exercise of power. Nor is he saying that people belonging to this age literally worship the Devil (a few do, but they are the exception). Paul's point is that Satan has a supernatural grip on the world during this age of sin and death. By succumbing to his temptations and emulating his prideful disdain for the will of the true God, we allow Satan to usurp the place of God in our lives, both individually and as a community. The result is spiritual blindness and death.

Satan Is My Name, Tempting Is My Game

What does the Devil do? By far his number one activity, at least where human beings are concerned, is temptation. Both Old and New Testaments consistently represent Satan as the tempter.

Satan was responsible for the first recorded temptation in the Bible. The "serpent" that tempted Eve to eat of the forbidden tree in the Garden of Eden (Gen. 3:1–7) in some way represented the Devil. It is true that Genesis does not actually refer to the serpent by the name Satan. However, the serpent was a common image in the ancient Near East for the god of the underworld (in other words, the god of death), for specific popular deities like Baal, and more generally for chaos.[4]

Genesis describes the serpent as the craftiest of God's creatures (Gen. 3:1) and reports that the serpent tempted Eve to disobey God (3:4–5). The cultural context, then, as well as the particulars of the passage, supports the Bible's later explanation that the serpent was the Devil or at least the Devil's instrument (Rev. 12:9; 20:2; cf. 2 Cor. 11:3, 14).

The rest of the Old Testament shows Satan continuing this same strategy to drive a wedge between human beings and God. Satan's intent in causing Job to suffer was to tempt him to curse God (Job 1:11; 2:5). Satan also tempted King David to take a census of Israel (1 Chron. 21:1), apparently because David wanted some assurance of the strength of his potential army (21:5). As reasonable as this may sound, what Satan actually tempted David to do was to put his trust in his human army instead of in God, as he had done earlier in his career.[5]

In the opening pages of the Gospels, Satan tempted Jesus to seek universal power apart from God's purposes, which for Jesus included suffering and dying (Matt. 4:1–11; Mark 1:12–13; Luke 4:1–13).

Later Jesus explicitly said that Satan was the source of the thought of not suffering and dying on our behalf (Matt. 16:21–23).

Both the New Testament epistles (e.g., 1 Cor. 7:5) and the book of Revelation (Rev. 2:10) warn about the temptations of Satan. The purpose of the apparent miracles that Satan engineers is to get people to accept a lie (2 Thess. 2:9–10). Revelation speaks of the Devil as the one "who deceives the whole world" (Rev. 12:9; see also 20:10).

Ironically, many people twist the biblical teaching about the Devil's role in temptation into an excuse for sin. The Devil can tempt you, but the Devil cannot make you do anything. (Sorry, Flip Wilson!) Furthermore, ever since we fell from our original innocence, temptations generally appeal to our own selfish desires and attitudes. As James says, "Each one is tempted when he is carried away and enticed by his own lust" (James 1:14 NASB). The Devil's role in tempting us to sin, then, does not diminish our responsibility in the matter. It's still our fault.

Whatever the Devil does, in other words, his purpose is to deceive us. His game plan is to tempt us to abandon our trust in God and to disobey him. Whenever we are tempted to turn away from God, we are listening to a diabolical lie. This is something everyone needs to know about the Devil.

SENSE

The Devil is a powerful, scheming liar out to tempt us.

NONSENSE

The Devil knows our every thought and can do anything.

Chapter 19

THE CASE OF THE DEVIL'S DOWNFALL

The Devil evidently is a fallen angel, but how or when he fell is a mystery.

How did Satan come to be Satan, the Adversary? The only answer that makes any sense biblically is that Satan was an angel God had created but who then rebelled against God. It is a fundamental truth of the Bible that God created everything, both in the visible, physical world and in the invisible, spiritual realm (Gen. 1:1; John 1:3; Col. 1:16). Satan must have been among the spiritual beings God created. It is equally fundamental to biblical teaching that God created everything good (Gen. 1:31; Ps. 104:24; 1 Tim. 4:4). Logically, it follows that Satan rebelled against God and fell from his original created innocence.

Oddly enough, the Bible never talks directly about Satan's fall. As much as this mystery piques our curiosity, the Lord has chosen not to reveal to us how Satan fell. Perhaps we would not understand—or perhaps we are just not ready to know what happened.

King of Babylon—the Morning Star?

Many people think that two poetic passages in the Old Testament prophetic books describe Satan's fall. The first is in Isaiah 14, where Isaiah delivers a scathing prophecy "against the king of Babylon" (Isa. 14:4). The prophecy speaks of God's breaking the king's scepter that he used to oppress the peoples (vv. 5–6). The earth rejoices at his humiliation, and the inhabitants of Sheol, the realm of the dead, eagerly anticipate the king joining them (vv. 7–11). Then Isaiah says,

> How you are fallen from heaven,
>   O Day Star, son of Dawn!
> How you are cut down to the ground,
>   you who laid the nations low!
> You said in your heart,
>   "I will ascend to heaven;
> I will raise my throne
>   above the stars of God;
> I will sit on the mount of assembly
>   on the heights of Zaphon;
> I will ascend above the tops of the clouds;
>   I will make myself like the Most High."
> But you are brought down to Sheol,
>   to the depths of the Pit.
> Those who see you will stare at you,
>   and ponder over you:
> "Is this the man who made the earth tremble...?"
>   (Isa. 14:12–16)

Historically, Christians have read this prophecy as looking beyond the human king of Babylon to the Devil. In fact, one of his most popular names derives from this passage. The Latin Vulgate translated the Hebrew word *heylel*, which meant "shining one" or "star" (v. 12), as "Lucifer"—a translation retained in the NKJV. However, if we take verses 12–15 in context, they appear to refer to the human king of Babylon, as does the rest of the prophecy (vv. 4–21).

Isaiah addresses this prophecy directly to the king of Babylon (Isa. 14:4), and specifically refers to him as a "man" (v. 16). But the prophecy also draws on pagan mythology to depict the king's fall from power. For example, in one Canaanite myth a god named Athtar (meaning something like "son of Dawn" or morning star) wanted to rule on Baal's throne from Zaphon, a sacred mountain of the north (compare "the north" in v. 13 in the NASB with "Zaphon" in the NRSV).

Most modern scholars, therefore, understand the prophecy in one of two ways. Some argue that the entire prophecy refers only to the human king, using religious imagery typical for that time to describe his humiliation. If this is correct, the king is called "morning star" (v. 12 NIV) simply as a metaphor that describes him as shining brightly only for a short time.[1] Others argue that the religious imagery implies that the human king's fall from power is an earthly picture of a spiritual event — the fall from power of a heavenly being. If this is correct, Isaiah is not endorsing the local pagan mythologies, but he is using them to convey the idea that behind the coming defeat of Israel's human enemies is the defeat of their even more powerful spiritual enemies.[2] If this approach is correct, however, it does not follow that Isaiah is alluding to "Lucifer's" *original* fall from innocence. More likely, he is intimating his future, final defeat.[3]

King of Tyre — the Cherub That Fell?

A similar question arises in Ezekiel 28, another prophecy of the fall from power of a pagan king and enemy of Israel — in this case, the king of Tyre. The chapter actually contains two prophetic messages, or oracles, against him. The first addresses "the prince of Tyre" (v. 2):

> Because your heart is lifted up
> And you have said, "I am a god,
> I sit in the seat of gods
> In the heart of the seas";
> Yet you are a man and not God....
> By your great wisdom, by your trade
> You have increased your riches
> And your heart is lifted up because of your riches....
> "Therefore, behold, I will bring strangers upon you,
> The most ruthless of the nations....
> They will bring you down to the pit,
> And you will die the death of those who are slain
> In the heart of the seas.
> Will you still say, 'I am a god,'
> In the presence of your slayer,
> Though you are a man and not God,
> In the hands of those who wound you?" (Ezek. 28:2–9 NASB)

It is clear in this first prophecy that the leader of Tyre is a human ruler, though he arrogantly thinks of himself as a god. Ezekiel states twice that the ruler is a "man." Evidently he made himself so rich through trade that he became quite full of himself!

But the second oracle from the very beginning seems to point beyond the human king:

> You had the seal of perfection,
> Full of wisdom and perfect in beauty.
> You were in Eden, the garden of God....
> You were the anointed cherub who covers,
> And I placed you *there*.[4]
> You were on the holy mountain of God;
> You walked in the midst of the stones of fire.
> You were blameless in your ways
> From the day you were created
> Until unrighteousness was found in you.
> By the abundance of your trade
> You were internally filled with violence,
> And you sinned;
> Therefore I have cast you as profane
> From the mountain of God.
> And I have destroyed you, O covering cherub,
> From the midst of the stones of fire.
> Your heart was lifted up because of your beauty;
> You corrupted your wisdom by reason of your splendor....
> By the multitude of your iniquities,
> In the unrighteousness of your trade
> You profaned your sanctuaries. (Ezek. 28:12–13a, 14–16, 18a NASB).

That the human ruler or "king of Tyre" (Ezek. 28:12) is still the subject of this prophecy is apparent from the reference to his unjust trading practices (v. 18), which the first oracle also mentioned as the source of the king's wealth. The description of this king as originally wise, beautiful, and perfectly blameless—and living in Eden—suggests a comparison with the fall of Adam, not of Satan.[5] What has led interpreters in the past to equate this king with Satan is the fact that the Hebrew text appears to refer to him as a "cherub"

(vv. 14, 16). However, the Septuagint, an ancient Greek translation of the Old Testament, says that he was "*with* the cherub who covers" (v. 14) and that this cherub brought him out (v. 16). Most biblical scholars today think this is what the Hebrew originally said and accept the Septuagint reading as correct. The NRSV, for example, translates these statements as follows: "With an anointed cherub as guardian I placed you ... the guardian cherub drove you out from among the stones of fire."[6]

The bottom line is that neither Isaiah 14 nor Ezekiel 28 clearly refers to the fall of Satan from his original innocence. We can surmise that Satan fell for reasons similar to those of the kings of Tyre and Babylon—arrogance or pride, and in particular the desire to be like God or to be a god himself. This makes sense when we note that the serpent's temptation of Eve and Adam in Eden was that they could become "like God" (Gen. 3:5).

The Day the Devil Fell

Just as we don't know *how* the Devil became a cosmic rebel, we also don't know *when* this took place. From Genesis 3:1–7 we may safely infer that Satan fell before human beings did. That is about the extent of our information. Genesis 1:31 says that God regarded everything he had made as "very good," and this suggests that Satan had not yet gone bad. But it is possible that Genesis 1:31 is referring only to the physical creation (since Gen. 1 says nothing explicitly about angels or other spiritual beings). Some theologians have speculated that Satan became jealous of human beings because God had made them in his image and ordained them to exercise dominion on his behalf (1:26–28). That is a possibility, but we have no way of proving it.

Another theory, usually called the "gap" or "restitution" theory, proposes that Satan fell before the creation events of Genesis 1:3–31 took place. According to this theory, Satan's rebellion ruined the original creation (1:1–2), and the creation events of 1:3–31 were actually works of restoring creation to a good, though not perfect, state.

The gap theory has some able defenders,[7] but there are some telling reasons to reject it. Genesis 1 ends on a far more positive note—that with respect to everything God had made, "it was very good" (1:31)—than one would expect if the earth were a partially restored, spiritual battle zone. Genesis 1 not only fails to mention any cosmic rebellion or supernatural enemy, it describes God's work of creation in tranquil, peaceful terms. God effortlessly speaks and light and dark separate, land and seas separate, plants emerge, animals populate the earth, and, finally, God makes human beings. God's instructions to Adam and Eve are to exercise dominion over the flora and fauna (1:26–28), not over the Devil and his demons. If Genesis 1 recounts the preparation of the earth and of humanity for spiritual battle, it does so in code.

The main argument in support of the gap theory is the description of the earth's condition as "formless and void" (1:2). Elsewhere the Bible denies that God created the world in such a condition (Isa. 45:18), a fact that advocates emphasize proves that Genesis 1:2 must describe creation in a ruined state. However, Isaiah 45:18 may simply mean that God did not stop at the early stage of creation and leave it unformed and empty, but continued his creative work until it was "very good." Thus, Genesis 1:2 may describe initial or early conditions of creation as a work in progress.

The evidence for the gap theory is too tenuous, then, to be the basis for any definite conclusions about the fall of Satan or the nature of the spiritual "war" in which we find ourselves.[8] That we are at war, spiritually, is clear; that God created us to be soldiers in a spiritual war that was already under way is at best speculative.

SENSE
The Devil is a creature who rebelled against God.

NONSENSE
We can know when, how, and why the Devil fell.

Chapter 20

THE WINDS OF WAR

It's time to separate fad from fact about spiritual warfare.

Spiritual warfare" has been a hot topic among Christians since the publication in 1986 of Frank Peretti's fiction bestseller, *This Present Darkness*.[1] Peretti's book started another trend still with us, the popularity of Christian "thriller" fiction such as the *Left Behind* books.[2] That is how many people see spiritual warfare: as an exciting, thrilling, heart-pounding adventure.

Sometimes it is. However, just as physical warfare often involves long periods of training, deployment, inspection, and simply waiting—a lot of which is unexciting to the point of tedium—spiritual warfare is thrilling only on rare occasions. Those exciting moments in the spiritual war can also be the most dangerous.

The Enemy

If we are to understand the nature of the spiritual warfare going on in our world, we must know the enemy. The classic statement in Scripture on this subject is Paul's remark to the Ephesian Christians (from which Peretti took the title of his book): "For our struggle is not against enemies of blood and flesh, but against the rulers, against the authorities, against the cosmic powers of this present darkness, against the spiritual forces of evil in the heavenly places" (Eph. 6:12).

We have run into some of the terms Paul uses here before when we looked at the medieval system of angelic hierarchies (see ch. 12). These "rulers" and "authorities" are not exalted angels in heaven but "cosmic powers" or "spiritual forces" of evil.

An alternate, modern misunderstanding of the powers identifies them as the "structures" of human existence, such as social, economic, and political institutions and systems. An influential variation of this view, developed by Walter Wink, identifies the powers as the "inner spirit" or spiritual force of such public structures or institutions.[3] As Clinton Arnold points out, this creative interpretation simply does not fit the cultural and religious context in which Paul and other biblical writers used these terms. Popular Jewish and pagan Greek writings of the period spoke of rulers, authorities, thrones, and powers as angels or spiritual beings. These spiritual rulers did exert influence over human institutions, but they were not mere symbols for those public structures.[4]

We should not miss Paul's statement that "our struggle is not against enemies of blood and flesh." The obvious meaning is that we do not advance our cause in spiritual warfare by physically attacking other people. A more subtle point—one that escapes too many of us—also needs to be made. One of the most common complaints that critics of Christianity make is that Christians tend to "demonize" other people. That is, many of us routinely refer to people of other religions, or other cultures, or other political parties, or even other Christian denominations or theological points of view, as "demonic" or "of the Devil." We often construe spiritual warfare to be a spiritual battle of *us* (the true Christians) versus *them* (the heretics, liberals, Muslims, New Agers, and so on).

There are some half-truths here, for false religions, heresies, and other destructive errors *are* demonic lies (e.g., 1 Cor. 10:20; 2 Cor. 11:3–4; 1 Tim. 4:1); some people *are* wholly captive to the Devil's will (1 Tim. 5:15; 2 Tim. 2:26); and some people *are*, like the Devil, scheming, deceitful opponents of Christianity (Eph. 4:14; 2 Tim. 4:14–15). However, the Bible does not teach us to view everyone outside the Christian faith (let alone everyone outside our particular denomination or theological tradition) as our spiritual enemies.

Like so many of us before we came to Christ, they need our help, our good will, and our love. We should approach people who do not yet know the Lord with a message of spiritual liberation. At the same time, we must recognize that we ourselves sometimes "make room for the devil" (Eph. 4:27) and thus think and act in ways that are more demonic than godly. Sometimes, *we* are the problem.

The Enemy's Objective

You might be wondering: Just what are Satan and his demonic powers hoping to accomplish? What do they possibly have to gain—and how can the Devil imagine that he can succeed in his rebellion against the almighty God?

Just as Scripture does not inform us as to how, why, or when Satan fell, it also does not tell us what he hopes to accomplish by continuing his rebellion. One guess is that Satan is trying to sway as many people as possible his way in the belief that if he gets enough support God will have to accede to his demands. As the Devil puts it in George Bernard Shaw's play *Man and Superman*, he may think that he will "win in the long run by sheer weight of public opinion."[5]

However, it is just as likely that the Devil and his minions are insanely angry. They may be striking out in blind hatred of God and contempt for humanity, seeking, like the thief of which Jesus spoke, "to steal and kill and destroy" (John 10:10). The apostle Peter describes the Devil as prowling around "like a roaring lion, seeking someone to devour" (1 Peter 5:8 NASB). Each soul destroyed may be no more to the Devil than his next meal.

> Each soul destroyed may be no more to the Devil than his next meal.

What is clear from Scripture is that these forces of evil are single-minded in their opposition to God. They are determined to pervert everything that is good, to corrupt everything that is noble, and to debase everything that is holy. Satan and his demons are out to cause as much damage to God's people and God's reputation as they can inflict, regardless of the consequences. They are the ultimate terrorist network.

The Enemy's Tactics

The powers of darkness engage in warfare against humanity in a bewildering variety of ways. We will look at the major kinds of demonic activities, beginning with the most prevalent.

(1) *Temptation.* In chapter 18 we demonstrated that Satan's main strategy is tempting human beings to distrust God and disobey him. Classically, Christians have recognized three avenues that Satan uses to tempt people. The apostle John called these three temptation paths "the lust of the flesh and the lust of the eyes and the boastful pride of life" (1 John 2:16 NASB). Satan appealed to all three of these wrongful desires both when he tempted Eve in the garden (Gen. 3:6) and when he tempted Jesus in the wilderness.

The first wrongful desire, "the lust of the flesh," is the desire for physical comfort and pleasure—in short, *hedonism.* One reason why Eve chose to eat of the forbidden fruit was that she saw "that the tree was good for food." Eve wasn't hungry or in need of sustenance, since she could eat of every other tree in the garden freely (Gen. 2:16; 3:2). The fruit was tempting because it looked tasty. Let's face it, temptation would never get going otherwise. When is the last time you were tempted to steal some brussels sprouts?

Eve gave in to the lust of the flesh, but Jesus did not. In Jesus' case, he really *was* hungry, having fasted for forty days (Luke 4:2). After forty days, even rocks start to look good to eat, and the Devil tempted Jesus to turn stones into bread (4:3). But to turn lifeless rocks into bread is not God's way; that would have been magic, not miracle. Jesus chose to put faithfulness to God's ways over his own personal comfort.

The second wrongful desire, "the lust of the eyes," is the desire to have whatever one sees—in other words, *materialism.* Eve wanted the forbidden fruit, not only because it looked tasty, but also because it looked nice: she "saw ... that it was a delight to the eyes." For the girl who had everything—almost—the desire to have whatever caught her fancy became a trap.

Satan tempted Jesus with a materialistic ambition that many men have pursued to their own destruction. The Devil "showed him in an instant all the kingdoms of the world" and offered to give them to Jesus in return for his worship (Luke 4:5–7). Such an offer would have been tempting, even to Jesus, because it would have allowed him to bypass the suffering and death that was God's way for Jesus to inaugurate his kingdom. Again, though, Jesus chose to honor God, which of course meant refusing to give the Devil any such honor.

The third wrongful desire, "the boastful pride of life," is the desire to exalt oneself, to feel superior and self-sufficient—that is, *egoism*. Eve was tempted in part because she perceived "that the tree was to be desired to make one wise." Eve hoped to attain wisdom of her own, independent and even in defiance of her Creator. Ironically, Eve (and Adam after her) was making the most foolish decision in human history. There is nothing wrong with desiring wisdom; there is something very wrong with looking for wisdom in the one place that God said not to go. Eve's real problem, then, was not her pursuit of wisdom but putting God to the test.

Satan also tempted Jesus to put God to a different sort of test by daring him to jump from "the pinnacle of the temple." Would God fulfill his promise to send angels to deliver him from all harm (Luke 4:9–11)? This dare tempted Jesus to "show off" and to exalt himself before the world by such an exhibition. Once again, Jesus resisted the Devil's temptation.

What all of these temptations have in common is that they pervert good desires into attitudes of mistrust toward God. There is nothing wrong with wanting food, fulfillment, and validation; we all need these things. What is wrong is ignoring God's ways and purposes for meeting these needs legitimately. One of the Devil's favorite tricks is to get us to justify evil means by good intentions or ends (cf. Rom. 3:8).

(2) *Affliction.* One of the simplest ways the Devil has of tempting people to stop trusting God is to make their lives miserable. The Bible does not attribute all suffering to the Devil, but it does indicate that some suffering is a form of harassment from the spiritual forces

of darkness. According to the book of Job, Satan was in some way responsible for Job's losses of property and family members and for his bodily afflictions (Job 1:12; 2:6–7). Luke reports that one woman at a synagogue "for eighteen years had had a sickness caused by a spirit" (Luke 13:11 NASB). It is evident from the way Luke words this comment that some sickness, but not all (not even most), is caused by evil spirits. Jesus confirmed that the woman was one "whom Satan bound for eighteen long years" (Luke 13:16). Similarly, Paul attributed a physical ailment with which he suffered, his "thorn in the flesh," to "a messenger [or angel] of Satan" (2 Cor. 12:7 NASB).

Some Christians infer from these passages that we can free ourselves from bodily afflictions through spiritual warfare—that is, by identifying the affliction as demonic and claiming freedom from the affliction in Christ's name. This is simply wrong. Job apparently knew nothing about Satan's involvement in his suffering. The Lord healed the woman in the synagogue, but he did not heal the apostle Paul. What we should learn from Scripture here is that whatever the source or nature of our afflictions or troubles and whatever the outcome, we should trust in God. Job learned this lesson, and then God healed him (Job 42:10); Paul learned this lesson precisely by God's *not* healing him (2 Cor. 12:8–10).

(3) *Demon possession.* In extreme cases, a demon can "possess" or take control of a human being, effectively dominating both mind and body. This term does not mean that the demon owns the human being it "possesses"; the idea is one of occupation and control, not ownership.[6] The New Testament describes such persons as "demonized" (*daimonizomai*) or as "having a demon" (or an "unclean spirit"). Contrary to the conventional wisdom of modern critics of the Bible, the New Testament writers did not regard all illnesses, or even all illnesses caused by brain disorders, as cases of demonization. The Gospel writers distinguish between the sick and the demonized (Matt. 8:16; 10:8; Mark 1:32, 34; 6:13; Luke 8:2; 9:1; 13:32; Acts 5:16), and Matthew specifically distinguishes between "demoniacs" and "epileptics" (Matt. 4:24).

The specific cases of demonization in the Gospels typically include evidence of involuntary behavior; that is, the demonized people did things they would not have chosen to do. In one case, a demonized man lived unclothed in the local tombs, where he screamed day and night and cut himself with rocks; he exhibited extreme violence and such strength that he could not be subdued or chained. The "unclean spirit" spoke through the man, calling itself a "Legion" of demons, and actually addressed Jesus as the Son of God and asked to be sent into a herd of swine (Mark 5:1–20; Luke 8:26–36; see also Matt. 8:28–33). In another case, a man "with an unclean spirit" identified Jesus by name as soon as he saw him, and when Jesus cast out the spirit, it threw the man into convulsions and screamed before coming out (Mark 1:23–26).

As these stories illustrate, the demons generally recognized Jesus on sight and knew who he was (see also Mark 1:34; 3:11; Luke 4:33–35, 41). In another case, a boy whose father described him as a "lunatic" (*selēniazetai*, "moonstruck," a general term for those with epileptic symptoms) had been throwing himself repeatedly into fire or water—suggesting the presence of a malicious demon (Matt. 17:14–18; Mark 9:17–27; Luke 9:38–42).

In two instances, all we are told about the demonized individuals is that they were mute (Matt. 9:32–33; Luke 11:14) or both blind and mute (Matt. 12:22). However, immediately before Matthew's account about the mute demonized man, he tells about Jesus healing two blind men who approached him and requested healing (Matt. 9:27–31; see also 20:29–34). Matthew, Mark, and Luke all clearly distinguish between those who are blind, deaf, or mute because they have demons and those who have such conditions because of some sickness or birth defect (Matt. 15:30–31; 21:14; Mark 7:32–37; 8:22–25; 9:25; 10:46–52; Luke 7:21–22; 18:35–43).

The Gospels, then, do not display backward, superstitious thinking when they identify some people as demon-possessed. To the contrary, they apply this description sparingly and soberly. The common perception that medical science, and especially psychiatry, has explained away demon-possession is simply false. With regard to symptoms, demon-possession tends to *overlap* medical and psychiatric disorders. In other words, some cases of demon-possession may be difficult to distinguish (by their physical symptoms) from natural or psychiatric disorders; in other cases demon-possession is markedly different from any biologically based diagnosis.[7]

The Bible does not explain how some people become demon-possessed. The closest we get to an explanation is a metaphorical comment Jesus once made comparing the demonized person to a vacant house that the demon occupies (Matt. 12:43–45; Luke 11:24–26). The implication is that any human being whose "house" the Holy Spirit does not already occupy is at risk of demon-possession. Since most non-Christians are not demon-possessed, it is likely that other factors, such as heavy involvement in the occult, may make some people more susceptible to demonic invasion. Then again, the demons may not care to possess everyone they can. Possession involves a demon focusing its energies entirely on one person, and it draws attention to the demonic realm—and that may not always be in the Devil's interest. We should not assume, then, that demon-possessed persons necessarily bring their condition on themselves.

However a person comes to be demonized, once they are in that condition they are powerless to help themselves. Whereas most of the sick whom Jesus healed asked him for healing, no demoniac ever approached Jesus asking for help. Instead, a loved one or friend brought the demonized person to Jesus, or Jesus encountered the individual and took it upon himself to cast out the demon. Jesus never required a demon-possessed person to express any faith; indeed, he never asked them to do anything at all in order to have the demon expelled.

Keeping this simple point in mind can save us from a lot of nonsense associated with so-called "deliverance ministries." We recognize that there are demon-possessed people in the world today and that Christ has called and authorized the church to cast out demons from such individuals. However, nearly all deliverance ministries cater to a broad constituency of Christians who erroneously believe that they may overcome all manner of personal difficulties they experience by having the associated demon cast out.

A notorious example of bad "deliverance" teaching is the book *Pigs in the Parlor: A Practical Guide to Deliverance*, written by Frank (and Ida Mae) Hammond. According to Hammond, everyone needs deliverance: "Personally, I have not found any exceptions."[8] Although he admits that "we cannot put all the blame on Satan and his demons for our problems," he claims that "we can blame them for much more than we once thought."[9]

A perusal of the three-page list of nearly three hundred different demons near the back of the book suggests just how much of our troubles Hammond thinks demons cause. The list includes such common human failings as resentment, stubbornness, bickering, faultfinding, envy, procrastination, pride, self-righteousness, greed, and gossip. Every cult and false religion has its own demon or demons. (Again, demons no doubt helped to inspire cults and false religions in the first place, at least through their work of tempting people to mistrust God and his Word. Hammond, though, is claiming that every member of these groups has a demon.) Also on the list are shyness, daydreaming, discouragement, headache, retardation, forgetfulness, heartache, embarrassment, sexual frigidity, and (gasp!) intellectualism.[10] We suppose that Hammond would diagnose the two of us as both having the last-mentioned demon. Ignorance and stupidity, however, did not make the list.

Hammond's teaching about demons and children is especially troubling. He implies that most demons enter a person before birth or during infancy. Most adopted children, he opines, "will have spirits of rejection." A child's stuffed toy frog could attract demons.[11]

We would not bother commenting on a book like *Pigs in the Parlor*, were it not one of the more influential manuals in the deliverance ministry genre. It illustrates that the church very much needs sober, sensible biblical teaching on demons.

SENSE

Demons tempt and afflict people today, including Christians.

NONSENSE

Everybody has demons.

Chapter 21

D-DAY: THE DAY THE DEVIL WAS DEFEATED

The Devil got creamed two thousand years ago, even though he won't admit it.

On June 6, 1944, Allied forces under the command of General Dwight D. Eisenhower invaded Nazi-controlled Europe. Over 5,000 ships and 11,000 planes carried troops, tanks, bombs, and paratroopers south across the English Channel. More than 150,000 troops swarmed the beaches of Normandy or dropped into French villages. The offensive succeeded but at a terrible cost. More than 4,000 Allied men died, many of them young soldiers on Omaha Beach.

The term D-Day originally stood for the first day of any planned attack (the "D" simply stood for "day"), but June 6, 1944, will always be *the* D-Day. The success of the Normandy Invasion ensured the final victory over Hitler and the Axis powers. However, the war did not end. The Germans did not surrender until almost a year later, on May 8, 1945, known as VE-Day ("VE" stands for Victory in Europe). Three months later, Japan surrendered on August 6, 1945, or VJ-Day (for Victory in Japan). Some of the most intense fighting and the highest casualties came between D-Day and VE-Day.

A Spiritual D-Day

What does all this have to do with the Devil? After World War II broke out, the German theologian Oscar Cullmann (1902–1999) taught in Switzerland, and after the war ended he also taught in Paris and Rome. Cullmann used D-Day in one of the most famous illustrations in the history of theology. He likened Jesus' death and resurrection to D-Day and the consummation at the end of history to VE-Day. When Jesus died and rose again, he decisively defeated the Devil. However, the Devil hasn't surrendered yet, and therefore the war isn't over. But one day Jesus will completely vanquish Satan and his demonic army. That will be like VE-Day.

In the meantime, we live in that difficult time between Christ's death and resurrection and his final victory over Satan. Although victory is "already" certain, the end of the war is "not yet" here, and "spiritual warfare" is in some respects more intense than ever. Thus, we live in a period of tension in which victory is in one sense "already" and in another sense "not yet."

Revising Rabbinical Theology in Light of the Resurrection

The Bible clearly supports this "already – not yet" understanding of the Devil's defeat. Paul's writings are especially rich on this topic, though the idea is found throughout the New Testament.

Prior to the coming of Jesus, Jewish rabbis generally divided history neatly into two ages: the present age and the age to come. The present age is the age of sin, oppression, and death under the domination of the Devil; the age to come will be the age of righteousness, peace, and life in the kingdom of God under the rule of the Messiah. In fact, the rabbis taught that the Messiah's coming would mark the beginning of the age to come.

When the Messiah came in the person of Jesus, though, he did not match the rabbinical expectations of the Messiah. Jesus led no mighty army against the Romans, as Eisenhower nineteen centuries later would amass the Allied forces against the Nazis. Quite

OSCAR CULLMANN

That event on the cross, together with the resurrection which followed, was the already concluded decisive battle.[1]

the opposite: The Romans came down hard on Jesus and put him horribly to death on a cross. Was this any way to win the war against the Devil? Jesus' death dashed his followers' hopes that he might have been the Messiah. No wonder that a few days later two of those followers—not knowing to whom they were talking—commented, "We had hoped that he was the one to redeem Israel" (Luke 24:21).

Yet the faith of those two men, and of a larger band of Jesus' followers, revived that same day. The man to whom they were speaking was Jesus himself! They had heard that some of Jesus' women followers had seen him earlier that morning, but they had dismissed the story as nonsense (Luke 24:10–11, 22–24). Now Jesus revealed himself to them, explaining from the Old Testament Scriptures that it was "necessary that the Messiah should suffer these things and then enter into his glory" (v. 26).

Yes, the Messiah was to be the glorious King who would eventually defeat all of the forces of evil. However, if the Messiah were simply to wipe all evil from the face of the earth, none of us would be left. Before coming in judgment against the wicked, Jesus came in mercy to save some of us from our own wickedness—so that we would not have to suffer the same fate as the rest.

About two years or so after Jesus' resurrection, a young rabbinical student named Saul was waging a one-man war of his own. Saul regarded the Christian message that Jesus was the Messiah as an affront to Judaism. He got permission to track down Christians in Damascus and imprison them. But on the road to Damascus, Jesus appeared to Saul, revealed himself as the risen Messiah, and told Saul that he was to take the message to people of other nations (Acts 9:1–19). Soon Saul was going by his Roman name Paul and proclaiming the message of Jesus to people all over the Roman empire.

Paul realized he would have to rethink some of his rabbinical theology in light of the fact that Jesus the Messiah, after his resurrection, had gone to heaven and did not immediately bring an end to all evil. The simple two-ages doctrine of the rabbis gave way in Paul's thinking to the idea of the two ages *overlapping*. The present age and the age to come are not neatly separated by a single event; instead, they overlap, with the age to come emerging in stages. This age is like the night, and the age to come is like the day—and day is near (Rom. 13:11–12). Although the day has not yet arrived, we should already begin acting as if it were day (13:13).

There is a good reason for this overlap. During the period between our spiritual "D-Day" (the cross) and "VE-Day" (Christ's return), God intends to bring many people out of Satan's kingdom and into his own. When Jesus appeared to Paul, he told the apostle that he was sending him to the Gentiles "to open their eyes so that they may turn from darkness to light and from the dominion of Satan to God, that they may receive forgiveness of sins" (Acts 26:18 NASB). Before conquering his enemies in judgment, God is calling people *to switch sides.* He offers to forgive our sins so that we will no longer be enemies of God's kingdom but instead be loyal subjects.

> The issue between you and God is ultimately not about whether you are a nice person but whether you are on his side.

For those who believe in Jesus, God considers this transfer of kingdoms to be an accomplished reality. As Paul wrote to one church, "For He rescued us from the domain of darkness, and transferred us to the kingdom of His beloved Son, in whom we have redemption, the forgiveness of sins" (Col. 1:13–14 NASB). In this respect, Christ's kingdom is already here as the result of his death on the cross.

Already – Not Yet

Although we no longer belong to the empire of the evil one, we still live within its borders. While Christ "gave himself for our sins to set us free from the present evil age" (Gal. 1:4), we nevertheless find ourselves still living in it. This age is still corrupt and under the rule of Satan, "the god of this age" (2 Cor. 4:4 NIV). We must therefore make an effort not to be "conformed to this age"

(Rom. 12:2 HCSB). We are to be like those Germans who bravely sided with the Allies, working from within to help bring down Hitler's Third Reich.

With his Son's death on the cross, God handed the Devil and his armies a humiliating defeat. Paul can even say that through it God "disarmed the rulers and authorities" and "made a public display of them, having triumphed over them" (Col. 2:15 NASB). Nevertheless, the Devil has not gone away. Christians must still be on guard against Satan, who will tempt us to live as if we still follow his lead (1 Cor. 7:5; 2 Cor. 2:11; Eph. 4:27; 6:11; 1 Tim. 3:7).

There is coming a day, however, when the Devil will not be able to fight any more. In the end, Christ will have "destroyed every ruler and every authority and power" that oppose God's kingdom (1 Cor. 15:24). He currently rules as the King in a time of spiritual war, and he will continue to do so "until he has put all his enemies under his feet" (v. 25). The Devil will be dethroned, death will be no more, and God will reign unchallenged (vv. 26–28).

Now is the time to take sides. All of us, from the most pious and moralistic to the most irreligious and worldly, are by default members of the Party. Not everyone in Nazi Germany wore the uniform, but everyone at some point had to decide whether to salute loyalty to Hitler or join the resistance. The issue between you and God is ultimately not about whether you are a nice person but whether you are on his side. God has taken the first move: "But God proves his love for us in that while we still were sinners, Christ died for us" (Rom. 5:8). Amazingly, "while we were enemies," God took the initiative to reconcile us to himself "through the death of his Son" (v. 10). He is still working, "behind enemy lines," to bring people of all religions, all races, and all nations into the kingdom of his beloved Son.

Jesus said that whenever even one person transfers allegiance from the domain of darkness to the kingdom of God, "there is joy in the presence of the angels of God" (Luke 15:10). You, too, can bring joy to God's angels. Make sure you are on God's side, trusting in Jesus Christ as your Supreme Commander to conquer evil in your own life. Then live every day as a member of "the resistance" (also known as the church), fighting against evil with the truth of the good news that Christ is bringing peace (Eph. 6:14 – 17).

You'll make the angels' day!

RECOMMENDED READING

Most people do not need to read dozens of books on angels and demons. However, if this book has whetted your appetite for more, here are ten books that we think are especially worthy of your time.

Arnold, Clinton E. *Three Crucial Questions about Spiritual Warfare.* Grand Rapids: Baker, 1997. Detailed, insightful study by a biblical scholar specializing in Paul's teaching about evil powers.

Garrett, Duane. *Angels and the New Spirituality.* Nashville: Broadman & Holman, 1995. Helpful work examining recent teachings about angels in light of Scripture.

Graham, Billy. *Angels: God's Secret Agents.* Rev. and expanded ed. Waco, TX: Word, 1986. One of the better books on angels.

Graves, Robert W. *The Gospel according to Angels.* Grand Rapids: Chosen, 1998. Nicely focuses not on the angels themselves but on what angels teach us about God, human beings, the Bible, and especially Jesus.

Guiley, Rosemary Ellen. *Encyclopedia of Angels.* New York: Facts on File, 1996. Useful reference work.

Kreeft, Peter. *Angels (and Demons): What Do We Really Know about Them?* San Francisco: Ignatius, 1995. Good introduction to Catholic thinking about angels and demons.

Lewis, C. S. *The Screwtape Letters.* New York: Macmillan, 1942. Delightful satire, in which a senior devil writes letters of instruction (and some rebuke!) to a junior devil.

Montgomery, John Warwick, ed. *Demon Possession*. Minneapolis: Bethany, 1973. Older collection of essays, many excellent, on various aspects of the subject.

Page, Sydney H. T. *Powers of Evil*. Grand Rapids: Baker, 1995. Excellent, scholarly study of what the Bible teaches about Satan and other evil spirits.

Rhodes, Ron. *Angels among Us*. Eugene, OR: Harvest House, 1994. One of the best popular books on the subject.

NOTES

Chapter 1: Angelmania!

1. David Keck, *Angels and Angelology in the Middle Ages* (New York: Oxford Univ. Press, 1998), 6, 29, 52. Keck's book focuses especially on Bonaventure.
2. Gustav Davidson, *A Dictionary of Angels: Including the Fallen Angels* (New York: Free Press, 1967), 111–12; Timothy Jones, *Celebration of Angels* (Carmel, NY: Guideposts, 1994), 175.
3. Keck, *Angels and Angelology*, 11, 34–35.
4. Mortimer J. Adler, *The Angels and Us* (New York: Macmillan, 1982), 101.
5. A myth some "experts" still perpetuate; e.g., Alma Daniel, Timothy Wyllie, and Andrew Ramer, *Ask Your Angels* (New York: Ballantine, 1992), 43. No one seems to know who first asserted that the medieval theologians debated the question about angels dancing on the head of a pin (or on the point of a needle, as it is sometimes put). Keck (*Angels and Angelology*, 74, 109) attributes the charge to Rabelais (ca. 1490–1559), a French physician and former Franciscan monk notorious for his attacks on medieval theology and for his generally obscene writings. Most scholars trace it back no further than the mid-1600s.
6. John Calvin, *Institutes of the Christian Religion*, ed. John T. McNeill, trans. Ford Lewis Battles (LCC 20–21; Philadelphia: Westminster Press, 1960), 1:164 (14.1.14).
7. Adler, *The Angels and Us*, 17.
8. Malcolm Godwin, *Angels: An Endangered Species* (New York: Simon & Schuster, 1990).
9. Sophy Burnham, *A Book about Angels* (New York: Ballantine, 1990).
10. Stephen F. Noll, "Thinking about Angels," in *The Unseen World: Christian Reflections on Angels, Demons, and the Heavenly Realm*, ed. Anthony N. S. Lane (Tyndale House Studies; Carlisle, UK: Paternoster; Grand Rapids: Baker, 1996), 2.
11. James R. Lewis and Evelyn Dorothy Oliver, *Angels A to Z*, ed. Kelle S. Sisung (Detroit: Gale, 1996), xiii.
12. "Beliefs: Trinity, Satan," Barna Research Online archives, *http://www. barna.org* (accessed 5/21/2003).

13. Terry Lynn Taylor, *Answers from the Angels: A Book of Angel Letters* (Tiburon, CA: Kramer, 1993), xiv–xv.
14. Philosophers refer to statements that are nonsense because they contradict themselves as self-defeating or self-refuting. For a simple explanation of this concept and several examples, see Kenneth D. Boa and Robert M. Bowman Jr., *20 Compelling Evidences That God Exists: Discover Why Believing in God Makes So Much Sense* (Colorado Springs, CO: Cook, 2002), 28–29.
15. Taylor, *Answers from the Angels*, 27.
16. Karen Goldman, *Angel Encounters: True Stories of Divine Intervention* (New York: Simon & Schuster, 1995), 17.
17. Karl Barth, *The Doctrine of Creation*, trans. Geoffrey W. Bromiley and Rudolf J. Ehrlich (Edinburgh: T. & T. Clark, 1961), 3/3, 369, often quoted.

Chapter 2: The Skeptic's Guide to Spirits

1. Adler, *The Angels and Us*, 42.
2. Boa and Bowman, *20 Compelling Evidences That God Exists*, especially chs. 3–8.
3. See, e.g., Gary R. Habermas and J. P. Moreland, *Beyond Death: Exploring the Evidence for Immortality* (Westchester, IL: Crossway, 1998).
4. See J. P. Moreland and Scott Rae, *Body and Soul: Human Nature and the Crisis in Ethics* (Downers Grove, IL: InterVarsity Press, 2000). There is a reason why we have cited two books in a row coauthored by Moreland: he is probably the leading Christian philosopher writing on the subject of the soul today.

Chapter 3: Never Ask an Angel for His Résumé

1. Robert H. Kirven, *Angels in Action: What Swedenborg Saw and Heard* (West Chester, PA: Chrysalis, 1994), 97.
2. See the entries on these and other alleged supernatural or mystical beings in Lewis and Oliver, *Angels A to Z*.
3. Daniel, Wyllie, and Ramer, *Ask Your Angels*, 173.
4. Jay Stevenson, *The Complete Idiot's Guide to Angels* (New York: Macmillan, 1999), 371.
5. Billy Graham, *Angels: God's Secret Agents*, rev. and expanded (Waco, TX: Word, 1986).

Chapter 4: All You Need to Know about Angels

1. Boa and Bowman, *20 Compelling Evidences That God Exists*, especially chs. 9–12.

2. We are excluding the Apocryphal or Deuterocanonical books, among which is Tobit, the book that introduces the angel Raphael (see ch. 13).

3. Barth, *Church Dogmatics*, 3/3, 410.

4. See Boa and Bowman, *20 Compelling Evidences That God Exists*, ch. 11.

5. See ibid., chs. 16–17.

6. Quoted in Jones, *Celebration of Angels*, 74.

Chapter 5: Lucy in the Sky with Demons: Are Angels ETs?

1. "Countdown to the Landing," *www.serve.com/unarius/landing/index. html* (accessed 12/30/2003).

2. DeForest Kelly, in the *Star Trek* episode "Bread and Circuses."

3. *The Urantia Book*, Paper 26, 1.1, available online at *www.ubfellowship. org/newbook/ppr026_1.html* (accessed 12/30/2003).

4. Geddes MacGregor, *Angels: Ministers of Grace* (New York: Paragon, 1988), 139.

5. Ibid., 140.

6. Adler, *The Angels and Us*, 5.

7. On these points, see Hugh Ross, Kenneth R. Samples, and Mark Clark, *Lights in the Sky and Little Green Men: A Rational Christian Look at UFOs and Extraterrestrials* (Colorado Springs, CO: Navpress, 2002).

Chapter 6: An Angel's a Person, No Matter How Small

1. The contrast between spirit and flesh is used in a variety of ways, with different emphases; cataloguing all of these uses goes beyond our focus here.

2. Augustine, *En. in Ps.* 103.1.15 (*PL* 37:1348, cited, e.g., in the *Catechism of the Catholic Church*, 329).

3. The expression "unclean spirit(s)" is found in Zech. 13:2; Matt. 10:1; 12:43; Mark 1:23, 26, 27; 3:11, 30; 5:2, 8, 13; 6:7; 7:25; 9:25; Luke 4:36; 6:18; 8:29; 9:42; 11:24; Acts 5:16; 8:7; Rev. 16:13; 18:2.

Chapter 7: Of Men, Women, and Angels

1. After we chose this heading, we discovered Kevin Sullivan's book *Wrestling with Angels*, in which he also uses this heading for his discussion of the subject of humans serving food to angels in Jewish and early Christian literature (see his *Wrestling with Angels: A Study of the Relationship between Angels and Humans in Ancient Jewish Literature and the New Testament* [AGJU 55; Leiden: Brill, 2004], 179–95).

2. The Hebrew text calls the two "the angels" in Gen. 19:15 and "the men" in 19:16, while the Septuagint Greek translation calls them "the angels" in both places.

3. However, the text does preclude the theory of M. J. Fields that all three visitors were "desert holy men" and that one of them impregnated Sarah! M. J. Fields, *Angels and Ministers of Grace* (New York: Hill & Wang, 1971), cited in Rosemary Ellen Guiley, *Encyclopedia of Angels* (New York: Facts on File, 1996), 2.

4. Although the Hebrew *mal'ak* and the Greek *angelos* can both refer to human messengers, in biblical usage these words refer predominantly to heavenly angels.

5. Philo, *On the Life of Abraham* 118; Josephus, *Antiquities of the Jews* 1.196–97; both quoted in Sullivan, *Wrestling with Angels*, 183–84.

6. Sodom and Gomorrah are notorious for their sexual sins, including same-sex acts (cf. Ezek. 16:43–58; Jude 7); see Kenneth D. Boa and Robert M. Bowman, Jr., *An Unchanging Faith in a Changing World: Understanding and Responding to Critical Issues that Christians Face Today* (Nashville: Nelson, 1997), 310–13.

7. For example, John Ankerberg and John Weldon, *The Facts on Angels* (Eugene, OR: Harvest House, 1995), 10.

8. The Hebrew reads "the bread of the mighty ones," using an expression that the Septuagint interpreted (probably correctly) to mean "angels" (Ps. 78:24–25 LXX).

9. See Boa and Bowman, *Unchanging Faith in a Changing World*, 267–71.

10. John Randolph Price, *The Angels within Us* (New York: Fawcett Columbine, 1993), 4.

11. Marilynn Carlson Webber and William D. Webber, *A Rustle of Angels: Stories about Angels in Real-Life and Scripture* (Grand Rapids: Zondervan, 1994), 48.

12. As Kevin Sullivan notes, "the vast majority of instances" of biblical texts referring to angels "omit any physical description" (*Wrestling with Angels*, 29).

13. Young men, we might point out, could appear "androgynous" (of no easily discernible gender) more so than older men or women of any age.

Chapter 8: We're No Angels

1. Sullivan compares Luke's version of Jesus' statement in Luke 20:36 to a statement made by Philo of Alexandria, a Jewish scholar from the early first century. Philo wrote that "when Abraham left mortal life," he "gained immortality and became equal to the angels" (*On the Sacrifices of Cain and Abel*, 5). Sullivan thinks Luke 20:36 "may reflect the same ˉnd of equality with angels, rather than mere similarity to angels as ˙rk and Matt[hew]" (*Wrestling with Angels*, 134). But Sullivan has

missed the major difference between the two writings: Philo was arguing that Abraham became an immortal and "incorporeal" (*asōmatoi*, bodiless) soul when he died, whereas Jesus in Luke was talking about God's people receiving immortality in *the resurrection* ("being sons of the resurrection"). The word "like angels" (*isangeloi*) in Luke 20:36 is different from Philo's expression "equal to angels" (*isos angelois*) and should be taken to mean simply that the resurrected people of God will be like angels in the way Jesus specifies.

Chapter 9: Angels Can't Hold a Candle to God

1. Goldman, *Angel Encounters*, 27, 33–35.
2. The saying has been attributed to the Enlightenment thinker Voltaire, though we have not been able to confirm that attribution. (Grammatical purists will note that "You are not He" would be the correct form, not that many people care!)
3. Janice T. Connell, *Angel Power* (New York: Ballantine, 1995), 68.
4. Goldman, *Angel Encounters*, 30, 31.
5. Ibid., 32, 33.
6. Ibid., 72.

Chapter 10: When Is an Angel Not an Angel?

1. Carol A. Newsom, "Angels [Old Testament]," in the *Anchor Bible Dictionary*, ed. David Noel Freeman (New York: Doubleday, 1992), 1:250.
2. Ben Witherington III, "Bible Q&A: Does the Bible Define the Trinity?" *www.beliefnet.com/story/111/story_11187_1.html* (accessed 1/10/07).
3. Paul may implicitly identify Jesus as the angel of the Lord in 1 Cor. 10:4, 9 (cf. Ex. 23:20–25).
4. Duane A. Garrett, *Angels and the New Spirituality* (Nashville: Broadman & Holman, 1995), 23.

Chapter 11: Jesus Is Coming — or Is That Michael?

1. For an in-depth study of the biblical teaching, see Robert M. Bowman Jr. and J. Ed Komoszewski, *Putting Jesus in His Place: The Case for the Deity of Jesus* (Minneapolis: Kregel, 2007).
2. Thus, a "chief jailer" is a jailer (Gen. 39:21, 22), a "chief priest" or "high priest" is a priest (Matt. 2:4; 21:15, 23, 45), a "chief official" is an official (Dan. 1:8, 18), the "chief (or captain) of the guard" is a guard (2 Kings 25:8–20), the "chief baker" is a baker (Gen. 41:10), and so forth.
3. A possible objection is that this particular compound noun, using *arch-* to mean chief or head, can only refer to one person at a time. However, some compound nouns using *arch-* can be used in the plural to refer

to a group of individuals, such as "chief priests" (*archiereis*, Matt. 2:4; 21:15, 23, 45) or "chief bodyguards" (*archisōmatophylakes*, Est. 2:21, LXX). This can be true even of nouns that appear in the Bible only in the singular, such as "chief tax collector" (*architelōnēs*, Luke 19:2).

Chapter 12: Name That Angel, or, Pin the Wing on the Seraph

1. See, e.g., Janice T. Connell, *Angel Power* (New York: Ballantine, 1995), especially 9–16, 177–238.
2. Keck, *Angels and Angelology*, 55.
3. Ibid., 60.
4. Augustine, *Enchiridion* 58, 59 (The Nicene Fathers and Post-Nicene Fathers, series 1 [Grand Rapids: Eerdmans reprint], 3:256).

Chapter 13: The Bodyguard

1. Guiley, *Encyclopedia of Angels*, 77.
2. On the Apocrypha, see David A. deSilva, *Introducing the Apocrypha: Message, Context, and Significance* (Grand Rapids: Baker, 2002). DeSilva gives a helpful overview of each book of the Apocrypha, including Tobit.
3. Ben Witherington, III, *The Acts of the Apostles: A Socio-Rhetorical Commentary* (Grand Rapids: Eerdmans; Carlisle, UK: Paternoster, 1998), 387.
4. Garrett, *Angels and the New Spirituality*, 23.
5. Eileen Elias Freeman, *Angelic Healing: Working with Your Angels to Heal Your Life* (New York: Warner, 1994), xi–xii.
6. Terry Lynn Taylor, *Guardians of Hope: The Angel's Guide to Personal Growth* (Tiburon, CA: Kramer, 1993), 13.
7. Freeman, *Angelic Healing*, 50–51.
8. Ibid., 88–89.
9. Ibid., 91.

Chapter 14: Sometimes the Angels Just Watch

1. On Jesus' quotation of Psalm 22:1, see Robert M. Bowman Jr., *The Word-Faith Controversy: Understanding the Health and Wealth Gospel* (Grand Rapids: Baker, 2001), 171–73.
2. Hyperbole is a figure of speech in which one states things in an exaggerated manner, not as a deception but as a dramatic kind of emphasis. The Bible makes extensive use of hyperbole. See Robert H. Stein, *A ⸱c Guide to Interpreting the Bible: Playing by the Rules* (Grand Rapids: ⸱ker, 1994), 123–36.

3. The Aramaic of Daniel 3:25 (Daniel 2:4b – 7:28 are in Aramaic, not Hebrew) says "son of *Elahîn*," which could mean "son of God" or "son of gods." (The same Aramaic word is translated "God" in verses 17, 26, 28, and 29.)

Chapter 15: Entertaining Angels

1. Doreen Virtue, *Angel Visions: True Stories of People Who Have Seen Angels, and How You Can See Angels, Too!* (Carlsbad, CA: Hay House, 2000), 161; emphasis in original.
2. Karen Goldman, *The Angel Book: A Handbook for Aspiring Angels* (New York: Simon & Schuster, 1993), 20.
3. Gloria Copeland, *God's Will Is Prosperity* (Fort Worth: Kenneth Copeland Ministries, 1978), 84 – 85, cited in Ankerberg and Weldon, *The Facts on Angels*, 38. On the broader belief system underlying Copeland's teaching here, see Bowman, *Word-Faith Controversy*.
4. C. S. Lewis, *The Screwtape Letters* (New York: Macmillan, 1942), ix.
5. Linda Stover Van Fleet, "Faith," December 8, 2004, *I Believe in Angels!* (*www.ibelieveinangels.com/staticxt/*); emphasis in original.
6. No one knows who wrote Hebrews. Despite the popularity of the belief that Paul wrote it, he almost certainly did not, since the author distinguishes himself from the apostles (Heb. 2:3 – 4).

Chapter 16: Putting Angel Stories to the Test

1. We are using "he" generically here. Women report a large majority of angel sightings; however, we take the same approach to the reports of both men and women.
2. There are other kinds of angel encounters besides seeing an angel (e.g., some people report hearing angels), though sightings are the most often reported.
3. For another use of this same kind of reasoning, see Boa and Bowman, "The Evidence of Jesus' Claims," *20 Compelling Evidences That God Exists*, 203 – 16.

Chapter 17: Yes, Virginia, There Really Is a Satan

1. See Boa and Bowman, *20 Compelling Evidences That God Exists*, 51 – 111.
2. Lewis, *Screwtape Letters*, 3.
3. Boa and Bowman, *20 Compelling Evidences That God Exists*, 113 – 26.
4. Probably the best known book representing this point of view is Elaine Pagels, *The Origin of Satan* (New York: Random, 1995). Pagels is an extremely liberal religion scholar who has written several books on the Gnostic writings (e.g., *The Gnostic Gospels*; *The Gnostic Paul*). The

Gnostics were an ancient heresy that professed to believe in Jesus but rejected the New Testament writings. According to Pagels, the Gnostics offered a more inclusive, accepting form of Christianity.

5. Michael Green, *I Believe in Satan's Downfall* (Grand Rapids: Eerdmans, 1981), 18.
6. Dennis F. Kinlaw, "The Demythologization of the Demonic in the Old Testament," in *Demon Possession*, ed. John Warwick Montgomery (Minneapolis: Bethany, 1973), 33–34.
7. Pagels, *Origin of Satan*, 42.
8. Sydney H. T. Page, *Powers of Evil* (Grand Rapids: Baker, 1995), 27.
9. Ibid.
10. Daniel, Wyllie, and Ramer, *Ask Your Angels*, 28.
11. Andrew Ramer, *Revelations for a New Millennium: Saintly and Celestial Prophecies of Joy and Renewal* (San Francisco: HarperSanFrancisco, 1997), 149, 151.
12. See Boa and Bowman, *20 Compelling Evidences That God Exists*, 151–87.

Chapter 18: The Details on the Devil

1. The exact meaning of Beelzebul is unknown; "lord of dung" and "lord of the dwelling" are the two explanations that scholars most commonly give (Page, *Powers of Evil*, 100–101). The translation "lord of the flies," similar in import to "lord of dung," is the basis for the title of William Golding's classic 1954 novel, *Lord of the Flies*.
2. Alex Konya, *Demons: A Biblically Based Perspective* (Schaumburg, IL: Regular Baptist Press, 1990), 104.
3. At least, this is how most Christians understand 2 Corinthians 4:4. A few have argued that Paul is speaking about a judicial blinding that the true God imposes on the wicked. The difficulty for such an interpretation is that in Paul's thought "this age" is an evil period characterized by sin and death, from which Christ delivers us (Rom. 12:2; 1 Cor. 1:20; 2:6, 8; Gal. 1:4; Eph. 2:2). "The god of this age," then, must be Satan, not God (see also ch. 21).
4. Gregory A. Boyd, *God at War: The Bible and Spiritual Conflict* (Downers Grove, IL: InterVarsity Press, 1997), 156.
5. Page, *Powers of Evil*, 35.

Chapter 19: The Case of the Devil's Downfall

1. See Garrett, *Angels and the New Spirituality*, 36–39; Page, *Powers of Evil*, 38–39.
2. See Boyd, *God at War*, 157–60.
3. See Louis S. Chafer, *Satan* (Grand Rapids: Zondervan, 1964 reprint of 1919 ed.), 18–19, cited in Page, *Powers of Evil*, 39.

4. The NASB italicizes *there* to indicate that the word has been added to complete the sense in good English.
5. Page, *Powers of Evil*, 41–42.
6. The difference in the Hebrew text is only in how the words are pronounced, since ancient Hebrew essentially used only consonants.
7. E.g., Boyd, *God at War*, 102–13. The classic defense is Arthur C. Custance, *Without Form and Void* (Brockville, Ont.: Custance, 1970).
8. As Boyd acknowledges (*God at War*, 113).

Chapter 20: The Winds of War

1. Frank E. Peretti, *This Present Darkness* (Wheaton, IL: Crossway, 1986). Peretti followed with *Piercing the Darkness*, *Prophet*, *The Visitation*, *Hangman's Curse*, *The Oath*, and a number of books for children and teens.
2. A series of books by Tim LaHaye and Jerry Jenkins that began with *Left Behind* (Wheaton, IL: Tyndale, 1996). The novels have sold over forty million copies and generated movies and other products.
3. Walter Wink, *Naming the Powers*; *Unmasking the Powers*; and *Engaging the Powers* (Philadelphia: Fortress, 1984, 1986, 1992).
4. Clinton E. Arnold, *Powers of Darkness: Principalities and Powers in Paul's Letters* (Downers Grove, IL: InterVarsity Press, 1992), 90–91, 194–201.
5. George Bernard Shaw, *Man and Superman*, Act III (entitled "Don Juan in Hell").
6. David George Reese, "Demons [New Testament]," in the *Anchor Bible Dictionary*, ed. David Noel Freeman (New York: Doubleday, 1992), 2:140.
7. See, e.g., T. Craig Isaacs, "The Possessive States Disorder: The Differentiation of Involuntary Spirit-Possession from Present Diagnostic Categories," Ph.D. diss. (California School of Professional Psychology, Berkeley, 1985); and the relevant essays in *Demon Possession: A Medical, Historical, Anthropological and Theological Symposium*, ed. John Warwick Montgomery (Minneapolis: Bethany, 1976), 223–78.
8. Frank and Ida Mae Hammond, *Pigs in the Parlor: A Practical Guide to Deliverance* (Kirkwood, MO: Impact, 1973), 12. Ida Mae wrote the chapter on schizophrenia.
9. Ibid., 22.
10. Ibid., 113–15.
11. Ibid., 117–18, 142.

Chapter 21: D-Day: The Day the Devil Was Defeated

1. Oscar Cullmann, *Christ and Time* (London: SCM, 1951), 84.

SCRIPTURE INDEX

Please note that boldface numbers indicate where major discussions of the particular verses take place.

ABOUT THE
AUTHORS

Kenneth D. Boa (PhD, New York University; DPhil, University of Oxford) is the president of Reflections Ministries and of Trinity House Publishers. His recent publications include *Conformed to His Image*, *Living What You Believe*, and *Sacred Readings*. You can find his ministry online at kenboa.org.

Robert M. Bowman Jr. is the manager of apologetics and interfaith evangelism for the North American Mission Board (4truth.net). His recent publications include *Putting Jesus in His Place: The Case for the Deity of Christ*. He coauthored two Gold Medallion books with Ken Boa, *An Unchanging Faith in a Changing World* and *Faith Has Its Reasons*. You can also find him online at biblicalapologetics.net.

We want to hear from you. Please send your comments about this book to us in care of zreview@zondervan.com. Thank you.

ZONDERVAN.com/
<u>**AUTHOR**TRACKER</u>
follow your favorite authors